Opportunity & Culture

- Four Decades in England

by

Manmohan Singh Maheru

First published in Great Britain in May 2012
by Merridale Publishing

ISBN 978-0-9572411-0-7

Merridale Publishing

Printed and bound by TJ International, Padstow, Cornwall

Contents

To my beloved countrymen, who somehow immigrated to foreign lands, yet are still striving to save their mother tongue for their children.

Preface

To immigrate to a new country brings with it more changes to a person's life than imagined. It is not simply that one has to learn a new language, if that is what must be done, but that one has to learn an entirely new way of perceiving the world. No one will dispute that leaving one's homeland to move to a new country is done primarily to embrace opportunities not available in one's own homeland but that also many unexpected events will occur in such a change.

The discovery of the human side of the new country is certainly a wonder; the history, the social structure, the daily small things that are NEVER mentioned in guidebooks because of the sheer numerousness of them. However, that also leads to an appreciation of what was left behind, in a way hitherto unimagined.

These essays reflect my own slow awakening to the experience that is England. Also, they include my thoughts and feelings of my own needs to hold on to my own culture and customs of the greatness of India, its language and literature in particular. I hope that I have been able to do that.

My thanks go to Alex Hamil MBE and his late wife Margaret, Uta Kliemann of Bielefeld, Germany, and to M. Kooner of Udasian, Birmingham, who gave

Manmohan Maheru, Alex Hamil MBE and Margaret Hamil.

Rainer Poralla and Uta Kliemann.

Rajinder Kooner and Mohinder Kooner.

me friendship and encouragement in publishing these essays. I am also grateful to Steve Gordos for his advice and for his help in proof-reading.

The writer is aware of the repititions, which were caused due to the similarity of the subjects.

Manmohan Singh Maheru 2012

A Life-Changing Letter

S. Mula Singh Maheru
(Father).

Karam Kaur Maheru
(Mother).

Manmohan Maheru,
14. Left winger of the
school football team.

Manmohan Maheru,
21 years on arrival to
England.

Manmohan Maheru,
23 years.

Mohinder Kaur
(Wife), 1944 - 1989.
A Community Language
teacher in Walsall.

Prof. Dr Carl Chinn and
Manmohan Maheru.

This was the letter I received informing me that I would be allowed to work in England. It proved to be a turning point for me as it opened the door to a new life in a new country and enabled me to achieve a measure of success in business of which I am proud.

BRITISH HIGH COMMISSION
CHANAKYA PURI
NEW DELHI 21.
5th January, 1965

Dear Sir/ Madam

COMMONWEALTH IMMIGRANTS ACT

I have pleasure in informing you that the Employment Voucher for which you applied under the above Act has now been received in this office.

The voucher can only be issued on production of your passport. Would you therefore call personally at this office with your passport, or alternatively forward it by means of the registered post. The passport and voucher will then be sent to you by similar method.

These vouchers are only valid for six months from the date of issue in London and your voucher is due to expire on 29-06-1965.

I would like to remind you to use the name and address shown above on all future correspondence about your voucher.

Yours sincerely

IMM. 229/11727/445324

MANMOHAN SINGH MAHERU
S/O MULA SINGH MAHERU
V. GEHLARAN,
P.O BEHRAM SAARISHTA
DISTRICT JULLUNDUR
STATE-PUNJAB
INDIA-144201

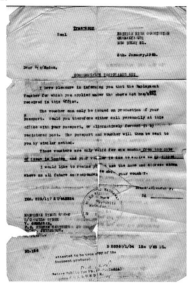

Punjabi Businesses in the UK

The harsh realities of life are that nobody can flee from his own family or country's history, and few people can ever escape the consequences of the past. We, the people of Punjab did not have much land for cultivation. Hence, the decision: either join the armed forces or emigrate to England.

The Last Prince of Lost Kingdom, Prince Duleep Singh, born in 1838 in Lahore. His father was Maharaja Ranjit Singh, the first King of Sikh Kingdom, andhis mother was Maharani Jindan. After the death of Maharaja Ranjit Singh, the British Empire brought him to the UK, where he spent the rest of his life. He married with Princess Bamba and had three children. He died in Paris in 1893. He left his palace and wide-estate in Elvedon, Thetford near Cambridge, where his graves established along with his wife Bamba and son Fredrick.

People kept trickling into Britain, one way or another. They made a good impression on the host country, which led to the Immigration Act of 1962. After this, the number of Punjabis in Britain increased. (Although Maharaja Duleep Singh could be the first Punjabi who lived in Britain for a considerable length of time, he did not come voluntarily.)

We came with the firm decision that we would work and work hard whether it be in the steel industry of the Midlands or the rubber factories of London. We were determined not to go back defeated, either by the molten steel or the stinky rubber.

Our motto was: ***We came to strike, to strive, to fight and not to yield.***

Few of us were financially secure, politically connected or socially established when we left India. Hence, we worked hard.

More than 1,000 angry workers walked out in May 1979 after it was announced the Auto Castings plant in Dartmouth Road, Smethwick, was to close with the loss of 660 jobs. Workers were joined by colleagues from associated plants in a march on the head office of its parent company, the Birmid Qualcast Group. Photo courtesy of Express & Star.

A Punjabi businessman now feels that economic progress and resurrection is the only way to survive and dominate both in India and abroad. Even the historical stigma of Punjab being conquered after Maharaja Ranjit Singh can be washed from his face. Hence, he works hard in business. This, I feel, is the background turmoil working behind our minds.

A Punjabi businessman cannot forget the corrupt administration in his own mother country. He escapes from a society that denies opportunity, disallows social equality, and restricts recognition and fulfilment of the native people. He is in Britain primarily to make money. No doubt, he has developed the habit of saving a bit and then ploughing it back into his business. Ironically, the harder work ethic of a Punjabi businessman further divides him from the indigenous majority community who are meticulous about holidays and work hours and resent both the infringement and the consequent competition.

Second generation Punjabis are those born and brought up in the UK, whose only contact with Punjab is through their parents. The enlightened educational system of this country has widened their horizons of thinking. They look upon Punjab with the same wonderment and despair as any foreigner. Born and brought up under the care of a welfare state, they cannot help taking sides with Britain. To them, Punjab is exotic, alluring, depressing, disillusioning, dissident and perhaps challenging – but it is not home. The country they

A Sikh Maharaja, His Highness Bhupinder Singh of Patiala, with Sikh and British soldiers.

Twice the Mayor of Wolverhampton, Cllr. Surjan Singh Duhra.

identify with is Britain.

If the people of Five Rivers do not change their attitude and the government machinery does not get cleansed, they cannot be enticed to return to their paternal homeland. At the same time, they have not forgotten the sad, sweet tales of their fathers who used to work in the Bermid foundries of Smethwick, Qualcast of Wolverhampton or British Steel in Bilston.

The primary difference between the British businessman and his Punjabi counterpart is related to how they start a business. In the Punjabi tradition, the financial aid comes from family and friends. The would-be businessman does not usually borrow from the bank or finance company but instead gets the money from relatives, who will loan him 20 to 40 thousand pounds. He then either buys a shop or starts a small manufacturing unit. The writer, at the beginning of his business, was advised by a local retired director to "trust nobody". But an Asian's start, on the other hand, is always with a trust in his friends and relatives.

It has been said that had the Mexican population relied on helping each other get a start in business, as do Asians, instead of the way they go about living in the United States of America, they would OWN Los Angeles. As it is, they are still second and third class citizens even after some 100 years.

HEROES AND WARRIORS OF PUNJAB
Miniatures on ivory with figures of Maharaja Ranjit Singh, Sher Singh, Dewan Dinanath, Fakir Azizudin, and others. Punjab, 19th century. Collection: British Museum, London.

We still have elements of a tribal society, we Punjabis, even though we have risen to a high status in the business community of Britain. A Punjabi will help another Punjabi, be it in a dairy business, a pub or other similar enterprise.

As Britain is the mother country of the Commonwealth, a Punjabi businessman has full faith in the system. The British are the most level-headed people in the world. History is witness to that. Revolutions can come in other countries and a few can imitate them but no one ever felt the need for such drastic changes over here. If justice is ever done in the world, it is done in Britain. It is in this faith in the grandeur of the British character that gives the Punjabi businessman the incentive to continue to work, to invest and to re-invest in this country. We know that Britain will never betray that trust and will never turn their Punjabi businessmen

Our advisor, late Gwyn Thomas of Pelsall, West Midlands, United Kingdom.

out with bag and baggage as has been done by others.

I do not claim this to be anything like an exhaustive study of Punjabi businessmen in the Midlands. What I've attempted to put forward are the different reasons contributing to the success they have been able to enjoy in their respective limited fields.

Lastly, there is a hidden store of goodwill in this country. It is our job to find it, harness it, and use it for our own betterment. The writer received unpaid assistance from a retired Englishman who brought over 35 years' experience in Black Country metal finishing to bear on the company's techniques and gave advice on plant, machinery and materials. We will always remain indebted to the 'Saint Adviser' and his home is always a shrine for us. In a nutshell, for every door that is closed, there are a dozen that are wide open. We, the Punjabis, therefore are confident that within 15 to 20 years, we will reach heights that our forefathers never even dreamed of.

Let me conclude with a bit of self appraisal:

"Brave men are we,
And be it understood,
We left our country,
For our country's good,
And none may doubt, our immigration
Is of great value to the British nation."

Written in 2008

The Role of Parents in Teaching Punjabi in London

'Gurdwara Nishkam Sewak Jatha', Soho Road, Handsworth, Birmingham.

"The Persians have destroyed our families,
O son, you've died of crying for 'water,
water' in the Persian language."
A Punjabi proverb.

Out of all the Punjabis living abroad, how many are those who do not wish their children to be one with them, to not sympathise in our grief and sorrows, who should leave their homes when they come of age and they should remain ignorant of their mother tongue, Punjabi? Parents always long for their children to be able to speak in Punjabi with them. So they should learn Punjabi and get proficient slowly. Parents want their children to speak with them and their relatives in their own language but sometimes their desire does not get fulfilled. Parents often give preference to their personal business.

Parents often get beguiled that if the children have discussions in English, they will improve it. In their heart of hearts, they think that the children are still living in India. They are not aware that there is English everywhere in Britain. Discussions held in English may improve a bit of the English but they will remain ignorant of Punjabi. Parents do not realise effectively that the rain and hail storms of English are already pressing them hard from all the sides. They will, anyway, learn this language automatically. They should worry less about that and should pay more attention to teaching them Punjabi, their mother tongue. While young, in nursery schools, they may lag behind in English; they do definitely lag behind. Not to worry. There is no need to get discouraged – personal experience in teaching and also the researches of the specialists are on our side. A year or two ago, these children did not know how to read or write even a single word of any language. In the next junior school, they themselves will jump on the horse of English language. In the beginning, and in junior school, you keep a constant eye on teaching Punjabi to them. All the linguists of the world are saying the same thing as the personal experience of Punjabi teachers in the schools.

Many years ago, I took my children from England to America for holidays. By enjoying ourselves in the sunny climes of California, we stayed a lot longer than the original holiday period. Contented mentally and relaxed physically, we returned from America quite satisfied. In respect of our children, we really earned our holidays. Surprisingly, you would ask me, how?

It was like this. My children, used to speaking both English and Punjabi at home, were soon surprised by the discipline my brother

Above left: The writer's sons Amandip Maheru and Yuvraj Maheru with his nephews Viramrinder Maheru and Neilinder Maheru. Above right: The writer with his children, Yuvraj (left), Dr Arvind (middle) and Amandip (right).

imposed in the house. Nobody could speak English in his house, whether it be his own children, those of his relatives or even of his neighbours. Very soon afterwards, my children emulated this. On our return to England, they have never dared to speak in English and all the personal conversations with me are done in Punjabi. This is also a symbol of respect for the parents.

My daughter's classmates often say to her that she speaks Punjabi like an adult. Her pronunciation is so pure that nobody can tell whether she hails from Verka or Vancouver; Jalandhar or Yuba City. It would be very effective to fix a minor fine for every English word spoken at home and also to give a little prize to encourage Punjabi. After taking the children into your confidence, try to use this magic method at an early age. The results should astonish you. It is best if done virtually from birth onwards.

Syed Waris Shah (1722-1798), a poet of eminence.

Sharda Ram Philouri (1837-1881), a pioneer of modern Punjabi prose.

In order to nourish plants and flowers, you need the right sort of atmosphere and fertilizers for them. Exactly the same applies to children if you want to increase their interest in learning Punjabi. Atmosphere! Punjabi atmosphere! Pure atmosphere!! All Punjabi visitors should be asked to speak in their mother tongue, Punjabi. There is no reason why they would not agree with your suggestion. Whenever they speak a word of English, your friends and relatives should feel as if a snake is smelling them from behind.

It will not take long to change the lifestyle of your home which in turn will cover them in the veil of Punjabi language and culture. You can make a start to addressing their future problems today, for the difficulties that you will face in the future would otherwise burn you like a firework. Otherwise, there will be no time left for repentance if you neglect it during your children's early years. When you realise this, it will then be too late.

It would be beneficial if mother, father and auntie – the three gurus of the children – take another decision right away. We are neither asking you to take a stand against a government nor are sending you on a Jaito front. We are asking you to boycott using three words of English – mummy, daddy and auntie. Just discard them like a peeled banana skin. This is a habit we can copy from our Pakistani brothers. It is never a sin to copy good qualities. The habit of eating together in a row, a tradition begun by the Sikh Gurus was a copy of the predecessors of Sai Mian Mir. In the three big cities of the UK, Bradford, Birmingham and Glasgow, Pakistan Punjabis are sticking wholeheartedly to two words – Amma and Abba Jan. The children love these two words more than their own lives. A Pakistani mother may be walking with a covered head in Soho Road and a Muslim Punjabi father may be dressed in a traditional Lahori dress but their children would always address them with those two words.

Committed to Punjabi language and Punjabi culture, Dr Kulwant Kaur of Patiala.

They would prefer death rather than use the word "Mummy" and would never insult their father by using the word "Dad". The two or three Punjabi words help create a cordial atmosphere in their family life.

After a bit of practice, you will feel the same sort of comfort in their usage. You are already using the two sweet words "Bha Ji" and "Bahn Ji". We are blessed with their constant usage every day. Bha Ji on the Beach, a movie, is already quite popular and has attracted audiences from far and wide. Being in English, it does not teach English to the Punjabi couples but does provide warmth in the evening, making them have a sound sleep.

There is another suggestion for the grandfathers. The role of grandfather has always been a matter of great pride in foreign lands. It was the grandfathers' coterie who took an initiative in Canada to fight the war of Independence in India. Sohan Singh Bhakna, Harnam Singh Tundilat and a man like Lala Hardyal heralded the slogan of independence for India. Is it not a matter of pride to regard a teenager – Kartar Singh Sarabha – as the Gadri grandfather?

Speaking generally, the grandparents in foreign lands seem to be wasting their time. Be it in community centres of Canada or the park of Southall or even the big kitchens of the Sikh temples, everywhere there is plenty of gossip, noise and ironic or satirical remarks side by side. If they are playing different kinds of card games in the newly-built old people's centre in Edmonton or in the

From left: Dr Gurpal Sandhu, Dr Deepak Manmohan Singh, Dr Ravail Singh, Dr Davinder Kaur, S. Balwant, Manmohan Singh Maheru, Kinder, Santokh Dhaliwal, Dr Sathi Ludhianvi, Gurpal Singh. Photo courtesy of Punjabi Quarterly 'CHARCHA' Slough, London.

newly-built Sikh temple in Sedgley Street, Wolverhampton, they still go through the Ajit and Tribune newspapers and discuss the politics of the Punjab. Everywhere around, there are hailstorms of English, but the self-created atmosphere in these places is no less than the village gossip centre. Yet, as soon as they return home, why do they look like a wet cat? Children are gripped by the TV and the grandparents just sit in the corners.

Some of the most progressive parents feel extremely pleased when they send their married children to their own new homes. They are forgetting here that just for their personal enjoyment, they are not only forgetting the advantages of a united family but also creating an obstacle to the children learning their mother tongue. Let it not be the satisfaction of their personal sensuous pleasures that governs their life! You may be trying to avoid the possible clashes of the newly-married or just trying to make the young couples mindful of their responsibilities. Or perhaps there is a fear in your mind that "the daughter-in-law will beat the mother-in-law behind the wooden cases."

The true resources of the Punjabi language and the pillars of Punjabi culture are really these Baba Bhaknas, who either stroll in the parks or roam in the stores just to look for a lost dream or hidden treasures. We can avail ourselves of them fully, especially in Canada and America, where they fly or follow their children fairly quickly. Grandparents are really the proper Punjabi teachers for our children, the resource of Punjabi culture. Other things being equal and balanced, the more time you can spend together, the better will it be. By having conversations with the children, they learn Punjabi and it gets sharpened like a knife on a grinding stone, especially if they start reading and writing it. Our opinion is that if they spend eight to ten years together, the children will learn enough Punjabi off them to keep them going.

It may seem a bit ridiculous, when we talk of the grandparents' role and duties towards children. Never mind, these senior citizens have done their bit by working hard, spending less, then saving a bit and settling in a foreign land. Others have dug even more deeply to keep the generations going. However, take a look at yourselves and your actions. Learn self-analysis. Being in foreign lands, you, unlike your parents, do not have to go for cattle food after a day ploughing in the fields, but you cannot get rid of beers and whiskies in the evening. It is a way of life for you to loiter in different public houses drinking. In England, even the public houses in the Asian-dominated areas have been bought by Asian landlords where the nightlife is worth seeing. They do not just drink beer, they flow it, they flood it at the back of their tongues.

The number of guests, has so much been on the increase that you are either the guest or the host. No end to that. "Come in, have a seat", and then very quickly, they ask like the tune of a song "you'll get

Prof. Mohan Singh (1905-1978), poet.

Prof. Puran Singh (1881-1931), poet and essayist.

coloured, homebrewed or British-brewed very soon". A moderate whisky like Bell's, which was a rarity in our times and still something special in many working class families of the British people, has become a thing of the past for you. You turn up your noses at that, but whenever it is suggested that you buy a Punjabi book, you seem to have a fit. There are plenty of books worth buying and worth reading by writers living in England. In the last three or four years, in England, I have tried to sell *Gurbani and the Contemporary Punjabi Culture*, published by Navyug. The Sikh temples of England did cooperate reasonably well, but these beer and whisky drinkers' priorities were always their alcohol – Black Satins and lager. A £20 note slips from their wallet very quickly like an egg, if it is Chivas Regal whisky, but their hand starts shaking if they are asked to spend £2 on a Punjabi book that is worth reading. They behave as if they were born with a silver spoon in their mouth. The truth is that before long they forget the memorable tales of their forefathers who are still alive and who could only get a third class home brew and no more than a drop of whisky at special occasions or festivals such as Diwali or Vaisakhi.

Our learned readers will think that we are deviating from the main theme, but that is not so. This is related to the main theme of teaching Punjabi to our children directly or indirectly. We will feel contented if, after discussing the duties of grandparents and the role of youths, we turn our attention to young married ladies. They are seldom contented with the change of dress from new silk saris to newly-designed suits. So how can they have Punjabi books? They are very fond of their make-up and clothes, O God!! They are not content with a suit worth £100 or £200. Their heart is not cooled down or in England, their heart does not get warmed up.

They are going against the tide as if the Ganges were to flow in the opposite direction – towards Pahewa. How will the mother tongue survive, if the Sarabha-type new youth do not pay heed to the revolutionary spirit of their grandfathers and the newly-married young brides do not listen to their old mother-in-laws' pieces of advice? During our times in India, when going out for a short hop, most of the women would have a pair of black skirts which they would put on very quickly on top of the everyday clothes. The folklore, loosely entitled "The pleasures of having a black skirt" or Ghagri, seems to have been composed during those economically low times. In a trice, young lotharios would take advantage of the minimal clothes the women wore. That is, it did not take long to undo them.

Our women workers in England are still very energetic and hardworking for they still sweat once they start the flour mills going. They never worry about whether or not their hair becomes dirty by accidentally falling into the cattle feed. In India, you may read about their performance in newspapers, but I know from personal experience that these women have increased production not by increasing the speed of the machines but with their own diligence and physical power. They have doubled production. They deserve our appreciation and congratulations. On the other hand, they like their glittering new dresses, possibly too much. They cannot maintain their status, unless they move to new houses, with the help of the same glittering dresses. If unable to do it during daytime, they make their dead-drunk husbands agree with them at night to buy a brand new home. As a result, they cut their cloth beyond their means. The deal is kept extremely secret until the house-warming invitations are slipped through friends' doors.

It has become quite a fashion to buy new houses. Influenced by the same rat race that relatives and friends are in, they take this major step without deeper consideration. It only results in them having to work

Guru Nanak Sikh Temple, Sedgley Street, Wolverhampton.

much longer hours than before. Out of a tiny population of almost 30,000 Asians in our city of Wolverhampton, more than half live in new or nearly new houses. It is a matter of pleasure and sometimes it looks honourable as well, but it becomes tragic when the new instalments of debt recovery sucks the life out of the newly-married couples. The result is a neglect of the mother tongue of their children and of the preservation of Punjabi culture in foreign lands. The older members of the community are also worried about it and some of them can only reflect upon their sheer helplessness.

The youth, the heroes of our second generation, do not yet realise that you can do without expensive whiskies, shiny drapes, saris, new sofas and houses made of new bricks; a minority in a majority community do not become great with all of this. No doubt it becomes a matter of pride and honour if you possess all of these luxuries. For 50 to 100 years, you can still carry on the line without them, but if you lose your mother tongue, or if you forget your culture, you are dying an unnatural death, committing suicide, are becoming metaphorically clean-shaven in total, even if outwardly you are Sikhs.

Sikhs, Singhs or beard and turbaned Sikhs, my immigrant brothers and sisters, you are still taking longer to understand all of that. You are still doing what you will, without considering the consequences and are spending money like water on your marriages – and that does not look good to the poorer Punjabis.

During the last quarter of a century, you have increased your interest in Punjabi music and folk-dance, Bhangra and Gidda. It is pleasing to see that you have fallen back to your traditional culture. At least, all of these entertainments are performed in your language by Indian artists. The respect and pride of your mother tongue has thus doubled. However, there are still improvements to be made. I remember an occasion at the beginning of the seventies when some of us were on our way back to London. We came with a Bhangra drum, a few other instruments and a Punjabi typewriter. People at Heathrow were looking at these instruments with great curiosity. We not only brought the drums to England but later played them and organised many musical concerts for a number of years. Many potential Punjabi poets and exponents of their own culture were gaining popularity. There was a Gursikh Singh living in Walsall near Wolverhampton, who always felt pride in his fancy dress and artistic shoes. There were not many who could sing Bhangra songs but plenty who could understand them. With their ears wide open, the audience would listen very carefully.

The audience would listen to the songs first and then some of the more interested ones would try to sing along with them. This reflected the depth of feeling for their mother tongue and folklore. During these days, you would dance and sway much more than they, even when you did not understand the wording or meanings of the songs. Some of the songs of modern singers are cheap, and at other times vulgar. Neither the pronunciation of the singers is correct nor can the audience understand anything due to the high pitch of the loud speakers. What I am saying is that it does not create a deeper impression, which should be the aim of these fine art musical concerts. You can not see your face in leather unless you first polish that leather well, with a bit of strength. It does not become a matter of pride, unless it affects your soul deep down. Some audiences are lost with the high pitch of instrument. Rather the bad affect carries on and is felt even on the second day. The main objective of Bhangra songs is to awaken your soul which is sleeping, so that on the next day, you feel refreshed, regenerated like a flower and not fatigued. The young audience sometimes take totally opposite meanings of the couplet but the pleasure is that they always look as if intoxicated and happy.

Dr Rattan Reehal, a writer; first to establish a 'Punjabi Literary Society' in 1962. In the same year, he was the first to teach Punjabi at Sikh Temple Cannock Road, Wolverhampton. Also first to publish a quarterly Punjabi magazine 'AMRIT' in 1963 in England.

According to their imaginations, parents use many other techniques as well, to teach Punjabi, for example movies or, while travelling,

From left, above: S. Arjun Singh, left India 1880, 1st Generation; S. Amrao Singh, 2nd Generation; S. Parshotam Singh Pabla, 3rd Generation.

Left: Mrs Harjit Kaur Pabla, 3rd Generation. Below left: Karminder Singh Pabla and Harkamwal Kaur Pabla, 4th Generation. Below right: Paramjit Singh, Taranjit Singh, Sukhjit Singh, 5th Generation.

Punjabi conversational tapes. These tapes prove very helpful even if you record them yourselves. Like approving a bride or bridegroom for your children, you should choose these movies very carefully. Choose the ones that teach your children correct vocabulary and which should give the genuine reflection of Punjabi culture, not the bogus, meaningless films.

Never do the couples or lovers stroll in our fields or crops with tight-fitted jeans. Never does anybody make these overt intimate acts in the fields, whether it be Sarin Shankar or Garhshankar, Rurka or Rurki. Similarly, the vulgar language of Ludhiana actor does not appeal to us much.

Parshotam Singh Pabla, an "Indian Jewel" prize winner is living in a half-acre corner house in Ednam Road in Wolverhampton. Their forefathers went out of Punjab to Malaysia about a century ago. Then they came to England afterwards. This is the fifth or sixth generation which are still proper Gursikhs; they speak Punjabi quite fluently and whenever they see somebody off, the whole of the family comes out on the road in respect. They have followed most of the steps described above. In any event, Parshotam himself is an old religious leader – of "turban action" fame, president of the Sikh Temple and a great collector of money for charities for the Sikh temples in Asia. He can interpret the Sikh scriptures and Sikh history, non-stop for 12 to 14 hours without drinking a drop of water. With a bit of care, everybody can be a Parshotam Singh when it comes to looking after your mother tongue. That is our firm belief.

Written in 1997

A World Class Punjabi Lady in London

The Congress, then, was derailed for the first time. Shocked by their defeat, some of the Congressmen came to England for holidays. During those days, we were sitting in a house in Birmingham, when Kailash and her husband Gopal visited it, Kailash, in an embroidered sari and Gopal with well-curled beard. The couple's faces were glowing with excitement. After dressing the emotional wounds of a young woman as an "agony aunt", when she went out, she was dressed not in a sari but in a suit. Be it a sari, a suit or her attractive hairstyle – it was all an indication of her self-confidence.

One, and only one, woman would dominate the headlines of the

Mrs Kailash Puri

Beatles of Liverpool, 1964

Punjabi newspapers in England – Kailash. Usually pictured in a sari with her hand under her chin, she was a showpiece for Des Pardes and an attraction for the readers. Around 30 thousand teachers who immigrated to England in the Sixties were her avid fans. They hung on every word, every line she wrote. Some of them would cut out her articles for future reference and others made notes of what she suggested. Off and on, she continued to make headlines, even in English newspapers.

Known as the "Sex Therapist", thanks to a magazine, *Sachittar Quomi Ekta*, published from the capital, Kailash was the talk of the town. Her column, "Sex Disorders", was read by virtually everyone and sometimes even prompted people to snatch the newspaper forcibly from their friends' hands. Brides, bridegrooms and all the young people would read it. She wrote constantly for decades. The editor, Rajinder Singh, was particularly pleased as her popularity increased his status. When he visited England, he promised, Kailash claimed, to pay royalties for her writings. She said he did not keep his word. "Didn't even spit on my palm", she said. After many years, he died and his death signalled the death of the paper as well.

Liverpool was the home base for the scholarly couple. The same city had once welcomed the Chinese and Jamaican immigrants and gave shelter to Jewish refugees. Liverpool, known for "world trade centre" and its seaport, also became synonymous with popular music. Foremost among many bands were the Beatles, who gained popularity and recognition with their long Sufi-type flowing hair.

Liverpool helped in spreading the race of blue-eyed people throughout the world, including the hard-working Irish, who had been living there for centuries. During the day the Irish built roads and houses and in the evening they would down pint after pint of beer, salajit-type, usually black Guinness. Roman Catholicism was their religion and they believed "no limit on children" was their birthright. The inevitable tragic result was an increase in the numbers of unwanted children A home set up by two local women aimed to send many of these unwanted children to foreign lands. They sent the first 75 girls aged between five and seven to Canada in 1869. Some 100,000 were sent to Canada and the same quantity to Australia, New Zealand and South Africa by ships. The children of these forced emigrants still visit Liverpool and England with reverence. A Dr Barnardo's Home, catering for such children was set up in Liverpool in 1892.

Be it a large or small house, it has nothing to do with creating the right atmosphere for writing. However, if a person hopes to be creative, a vast library-type atmosphere in your own house is of great value in trying to achieve something. Sir Francis Bacon, who died in 1626, was proud of the fact that he had 2,000 books in his house. Kailash and Gopal had a large collection of books in their Liverpool home as well and competed with each other in their literary output.

They did their writing at number 36 Merilocks Road, Liverpool. Never did they get tired of writing. Even when they would make a cup of tea or coffee for each other or would be busy looking after their front and back gardens, they would still have their minds on writing

It was an ideal couple. Their couple-power was marvellous as well and people would reveal their secrets to them almost as soon as they saw them.

The flag of "golden jubilee" was hoisted in Delhi. On arrival, there were invitations every month. Then they began a programme of visiting foreign lands for many years. They were quick in making decisions. For this year, they selected America and enjoyed themselves to the full. Gopal would play sexy jokes on Kailash's birthday and many days after. He was also very particular about putting on the suit of his choice. Alas, on their return from America, Gopal died.

They walked hand in hand with each other, only three days before. Two days before that, he asked especially to eat Choori (sugar-mixed chapati bread). Kailash herself combed his hair, pressed his forehead and cleaned his face on the last day. "A Learned Scientist Dies" read the headlines.

It was suggested that the writer should now leave Liverpool and move to Cheyne Walk in London. This is the place where thinkers, engineers, literary men and artists lived in the 19th Century. Even today, it is a favourite place of tourists. If ever the majority of literary men, artists or VIPs ever lived in a single street or road, then it is Cheyne Walk. Some well-known people can be seen strolling there with their cats or dogs even today!

The English novelist Mrs Gaskell was born in number 93 and another famous woman novelist, George Eliot, died in number 4. The engineer Sir Maurice Fitzmaurice lived there as well. He was one of the first in the world to construct a tunnel under water. He designed the Rotherhithe Tunnel, the first road tunnel under the Thames. In his heyday, even the painter Turner was attracted to Cheyne Walk and moved to number 119. Many poets and artists, including Dante Gabriel Rossetti, and Pre-Raphaelite poets lived in number 16. Today many famous people have their homes there.

They were told that their residence in "Cheyne Walk" could become a revered place and people would enjoy visiting it, like the Bronte Sisters' home. In contrast, only a trickle of people would be likely to go to Liverpool.

Some people revere politicians like gold. We evaluate our literary men by how they are valued by their contemporaries. How many women writers were there when Kailash picked up her pen? How many girl students were sent to schools? How many of them have faced the difficulties of immigration like gypsies? How many chose Sex, The Forbidden Subject for their writing until now? How many of them have tried their hand at subjects and gained fluency in many languages? How many have given lessons in cookery to the white ladies and how many have taught yoga to Asians and the indigenous youths? How many of them have hypnotised an audience of fellow staff and how may of them have participated in university debates? In such a long period, a literary person may have had some drawbacks but these should be overlooked.

What interesting prose Kailash writes. Prominent Indian commissioner, Chancellor Randhawa, was most taken with her style and would visit her in his jeep. She did not use nudity in her prose, even when she was writing about nudity.

Mrs Kailash Puri and Dr Gopal Singh Puri, cracking a joke.

In her article, A Blemish On Character, a very young girl – a baby carrot of a girl, as the saying goes – says to her mother: "My heart longs to meet a beautiful young man today. I should lie down in his lap after sucking the fire of his love with my lips".

Then note the writer's own comments on it: "This is what the British call their personal freedom and are pleased to avail it and that nobody can interfere in their personal life…Then what is the difference between a room and a virgin girl?" The answer – anyone can enter a room!

Note her writing style in the *Freedom of Sex* – "Nobody ever thought of going to the bed with somebody, when I was 17 or 18. Not just that, if ever somebody's arm would touch your neck in love, the whole of your body was shaken after experiencing its warmth and for many days after could be intoxicated with this experience."

See next, how does a damsel feel after passing through a bitter experience? "After this first sex experience, I feel repulsed and have here taken an oath that I would never go to bed with somebody unless I was married to him. I won't sacrifice the romantic pleasure and the pleasure of touch by going to bed with just anyone." It is the same tone in another article, Rape and Gratification.

"Some people enjoy spiritual pleasure by becoming engrossed in love and still others are destroyed by committing the blunder of rape". The followers of "true love" know how much higher and ecstatic this style of love making is compared with that crime.

Some critics think that Kailash speaks only of bed and sex. This is not so as this quotation shows: "After the marriage ceremony, performed in the presence of Guru Garath Sahib, the couple just married have two physical bodies but their respect for each other, love, harmony and thinking should be used in such a way that they could surmount the ups and downs of family life in harmonious living."

This is how she makes the British understand the importance of getting up early in the last part of night. "This part of morning is the time to become in tune with the Almighty by singing hymns and to thank Him for the blessings He has bestowed upon you. Rather than go mad through high-sounding pop music. By doing this you get peace of mind, balance, equilibrium and self-confidence."

What is it that spiteful jealous people do? "They only find fault in you. They set fire to you."

What then is the reality? "They don't become enlightened unless their thinking elevates their soul with sublimity."

Unlike Ajit Kaur – the bull under the earth being nourished in the capital – the writer does not claim a tenfold power in her arms, but does take the initiative where the rights of women are concerned in her article,

Ex Prime Minister Mrs Margaret Thatcher and Mrs Kailash Puri.

The State of Asian Women.

A memorable photo of Kailash with Margaret Thatcher was published in *"Des Pardes Weekly"*. The literary woman is wearing a sari and the stateswoman a skirt. Both were the same age and Mrs Thatcher was not yet prime minister. Although both middle-aged the two looked like sisters, a pair of doves. Tarsem Singh, the editor of the weekly, loved to display such photos in his office.

"Only he knows, who gets hurt" may be right, but there are many others in this world who can experience this pain themselves when they see others getting hurt. Some people just absorb it in themselves but others are able also to express it to others. When a literary man is hurt, he expresses it in an artistic way. A good example is how the writer recognises the pulse of women in *The Punjabi People in England*.

"The women covered their heads with handkerchiefs and kept their Punjabi shirt on top of their trousers, so that the scrutinising eyes of their husbands should remain tolerant. On one side was the arrogance of their husbands and on the other the curse of dual culture for their growing children."

I cannot end this article without giving a few more quotations:

"It was a necessity to learn English, but it could be learnt without sacrificing the mother tongue."

"It is a mother's duty to know that English is compulsory but it maintains your pride and individuality if you communicate among your friends and relatives in your mother tongue." From *Mother Tongue, Direction and Possibilities.*

"Mother tongue is the basis of your culture and civilisation; your recognition, your heritage and the richness of life. Anybody who does not speak in his mother tongue is refusing to recognise his or her mother." From *You and your Recognition.*

Now, should we talk of sense or of Manjit Indra's *The Shaj of Stars.* Shaj is a word similar to chaff as in the phrase "separating the wheat from the chaff. Then there is Manjit Tiwana, the poet, and her prize-winning *Savittri*; Ajit Kaur's *Gypsies* or of Amarita Pritam's astrology of *Three Heavens* or of Vina Verma who though thinner than a hair is sharp like a dagger and whose pen flows like honey.

Kailash did not let the pen rule her life. Along with being the writer of 30 books, she gave birth to three children and taught others how to become a mother; she held consultations, gave advice, reunited couples and saved them from the aftermath of divorce.

Being a mother is not the criterion for evaluating writers, but to destroy this gem-like birth just for pen and money is not a life. You must consider your

Dr Manjit Tiwana, a Punjabi poet.

husband but, after that, there is no need to get yourself imprisoned in your home?

Side by side, we also advise Parabhjot Kaur to go through Colonel Narinderpal Singh's new novel *Empty Earth and Skies – The Presentation of Impertinent Women*.

We can say with pride that if Sophia Loren, the Italian actress, taught the world the art of subtle love-making, then Kailash has at least paved the way for our men to follow. Good for her! In other words, she kept one hand on the napkin and the other on the pen and simultaneously rejoicing in life, drinking sherry or champagne, playing golf and chess, eating sweet and bitter, watching youth festivals of Gidda and Tiyan, and enjoying varied tastes of life.

We hope the grandmother madam will live for ages.

Written in 1996

The Millennium Dome of London

Millennium Dome of London, completed in 1999.

The first day of the 21st Century saw a crowd of two to three million in London. It was a moment, a special night in one's life – and not a honeymoon night, either – that was emblazoned in people's minds like a torch. They will carry on telling the tale of this night to their children and grandchildren.

Everybody had one eye on Big Ben of London and the other one on the River Thames. There was a variety of lights from many sides and at some distance. From London Bridge to Vauxhall Bridge, there were hails of fireworks, streams of Catherine wheels and skyrockets. It was almost reminiscent of Coventry but this bombardment was happening in

England's capital. It was as if London were burning, as if the river waters were set on fire as well. On that night, many children had travelled on foot. As sanitary accommodation was limited, many women and children were seen for the first time passing water in public!

All architecture, from the construction of the palaces of the kings to the spacious farm houses of the non-resident Indians or aristocrats, is symbolic. There is something more behind all this pomp, a living memory of the past.

In the days of the Roman Empire, Emperor Titus finished building the Coliseum which could seat 50,000 spectators. It is still intact. Shah Jahan, confident of his own empire, oversaw the building of the Taj Mahal and during the reign of Kutbudin, the Kutb Lath was built in Delhi.

As soon as the Sikh Gurus studied and analysed the philosophical and spiritual writing of their sages and seers, they confidently laid the foundation for the Golden Temple in Amritsar.

Before December 31, 1999, the Georgia Dome in America was the largest cable-supported dome in the world. However, the Millennium Dome in London surpassed it.

In the West, we consider years ending in zero to be milestones. This is especially so when it comes to the turn of the century and even more so with

The Coliseum in Rome

The Golden Temple in Amritsar

the turn of a millennium – or, more specifically, the year that marks the end of the millennium, such as 1000AD or 2000AD. The Popes generally celebrated such days after every 25, 50 or 100 years spans. In spiritual language, they are called "jubilee" years to inspire the masses. While 1601, 1701, 1801 or 1901 were celebrated it was years ending in three zeroes that appealed to the masses more than those ending in the figure one.

These three zeroes have a lot of importance in Christianity. When

Jalianwala Bag 1919 - Massacre of Amritsar.

you first see these three zeroes together, they touch your mind and then they concentrate your thoughts on the challenge in front of you, a very meaningful and a big solid challenge.

There are many other important dates in history, such as: 1492, when other civilisations began to fall following the discovery of America; 1919, the year which created momentum for the Indian independence; or 1947 the year India did get its independence. However, the three zeroes that mark the end of the millennium carry more weight visually than those years. It is a milestone in the march of history, regardless of specific events.

Before Christianity was established, time was measured only by the ruling periods of kings and queens. In London the tradition had been to celebrate the new year in the open air in Trafalgar Square around Lord Nelson's high pedestal. Would this be good enough for the birth of 2000? Two zeroes were to be replaced by three so why not celebrate in a big and majestic way? The question was: WHERE should it be celebrated?

We who ruled the world for centuries, we who ruled even the waves – where should we have the leaders, kings and queens of the world sit for that celebration party? Perhaps it could be in Caxton Hall or the Albert Hall, where Madan Lal Dhingra proved his determination to Vir Sawarkar? It was in Caxton Hall that Udham Singh of Sunam

The streets of Wolverhampton were lined by crowds turning out for the town's Empire Day Parade in May 1922. Photo courtesy of Express & Star.

Veer Savarkar (1883-1966).

Madan Lal Dhingra (1883-1909).

assassinated Michael O'Dwyer. The question was whether these halls were large enough. After all, Britain once had the biggest empire and the most powerful giant "Laat Sahib". "Flags followed the clergymen" was how most of the Christian empires were built. The British, unlike Alexander, did not start out with the idea of conquering the world. However, establishing an empire was almost a natural consequence of the paths made by Christian clergymen.

Christianity is still the majority religion in Britain despite the existence of many other minority ones as well. There are also many other Christian countries. Through their own empires, they taught as many lessons to other cultures as they could, even if some have since been totally extinguished. Should we not therefore honour such a religion? This is our pious duty!

So the decision was to build the Millennium Dome, which would

The writer's son, Amandip Singh Sukraat Maheru (March 1974-May 2011). The first Asian head boy of Wolverhampton Grammar School.

Sir Michael O'Dwyer (1864-1940), Governor Punjab in 1919.

also prove a major attraction for tourists. With the change of the century, people would pay homage to Britain and businessmen would fill their pockets and those already well off in London would get fatter and fatter.

The next step was to think about a location for the big event and ultimately they hit upon the ideal place. Because the world's time is measured from Greenwich, once a small village in London, it was decided the huge dome should be built there to ensure the third millennium, since the birth of Christ, would start with a roar.

It was decided that the dome would be built by the Thames in 130 acres marsh land. It would be the biggest dome type building in the world and would be the equivalent of 13 Albert Halls. The total circumference could be 1 kilometre. If constructed in the centre of London it would cover the whole of Trafalgar Square, the National Gallery and half of the Whitehall.

Pillars as high as 300 feet, or twice the size of Nelson's column in Trafalgar Square, would have to be sunk into the ground. Weighing 105 tonnes, these pillars would be like giant tent poles. The cables needed to support the dome from these pillars would be as long as from Lahore to Amritsar.

There are 12 of these pillars, perhaps symbolic of the 12 apostles at Christ's last supper. Like the Sikh flag (Nishan Sahib) of the Golden Temple, these pillars are yellow. Because of the red light on the top of each pillar, small aircraft can see them and ensure they avoid them.

Similar roofing material to that used at the Dome had been used for the two million square feet Japanese Toyota premises near Derby and the huge offices of the Inland Revenue at Nottingham.

The roof is not made of steel or cement. It is like a crust and is only 1.2 millimetres thick but, according to legend, it is so strong that you

General Dyer of Amritsar tragedy 1919 (1864-1927).

Jamaican-born Ezkeil Nelson, an excellent Wolverhampton-based metal finisher - with an expert aesthetic eye.

could land a jumbo jet on it. This is called "tissue engineering". Even the high rise buildings of nearby Canary Wharf are dwarfed by the far-stretching dome. That type of roofing was the most cost-effective at forty pounds a square foot. You could not get a sheet roof erected in England for that money.

The most skilled labour in England is spread around Wolverhampton, Birmingham, Coventry and Sheffield. How could Londoners, who seem always to be after money, compete? So the roof builders came from Sheffield and they did not take long to put on the cream-coloured roof. The Sheffield men stuck to the roof like spiders and completed it in a day or two. Within days, the dome was lit up like a balloon, as if a spaceship from the ancient Romans had landed by the river, very smoothly and without a jerk.

The dome has the capacity of about a thousand Olympic-standard swimming pools. Eighteen thousand of the double-decker busses which roar through London day and night could easily be parked in this dome. It would take more than ten minutes to fill up if Niagara Falls were somehow to pour into the dome. The Eiffel Tower of Paris could easily be stored in this dome.

A million square feet is the total area. It may not look so much from the outside but it looks much, much bigger when you go inside. Outside there is mud and damp all around. The interior? – it feels as if you have gone inside a giant egg.

Tirathe Hajj of Mecca, built with money from oil-rich Saudi Arabia, may look bigger but according to an Arab Prince "It is not under one umbrella."

The British are in no way less skilful. They may not be able to turn the face of Mecca, but if need be they can create a miracle.

In the centre of the London Dome, there is a 50ft-high stage – about the same height as Nelson's Column. The entire dome is four times bigger than the Coliseum of Rome. It is indeed a miracle of music, dance and aerial dramatisation!

The Millennium Dome Show, which marked its opening, told the story of a fictional set of beings, their transition from agriculture to industry and the segregating of different races. Ovo is the offspring of two races and is set to sail into the sky after a catastrophe occurs. The finale

Udham Singh Sunam (1899-1940) under arrest.

sees a beautiful tree, the symbol of new life, rises up into the sky. Mirroring the way people go to Mecca in droves on Hajj, we see 61 players on the stage at one time.

Another feature is a musical tone which was started on December

Two players of the show, Ovo, the offspring of two races.

31, 1999, and will carry on for a thousand years with no two tunes the same.

When some of the passengers at certain London underground stations come out, it looks as if they are taken out by individual lifts. However, as soon as they see daylight as they leave the new North Greenwich station, they must feel as if there is another

Millennium Dome show - an aerial performance.

planet under the stars and that there is another sky in front of them.

Whether it be poetry, Phulkary-art, the paintings of Kangra or the architecture of London or Egypt, we must examine it according to the times in which it flourished.

Before fast means of communication, architecture just carried on developing very slowly like the gait of a peacock. For a long time, few drastic changes took place. Starting from the Egyptian Pyramids, very little progress was made for centuries. Bricks and mortar was the material and the same style of architecture continued for thousands of years.

Then there was a change of trend in the 19th Century. The French Revolution came and went and then, starting from England, the whole of Europe became involved in machinery. There was iron and iron

Iron Bridge of Telford - the first iron bridge of the world.

foundries seemed to be everywhere.

In England, the first iron bridge was built in what is now Telford, near Wolverhampton, and the Eiffel Tower of France followed. Both marked a new trend in architecture. When the Crystal Palace was built in 1851, the British Empire was at her zenith. The palace took only nine months to complete.

In the modern age, there are new models every day and the individuality of our dome is in its usage of new building or roofing material. Some people look at our dome with critical eyes but they should remember that architecture is not something that comes from the sky. With changing attitudes, the architect can create original works through his or her imagination and that is what has been done here. Our dome is the result of new building material used in an artistic manner.

Written in 2001

The Oxford Street of London

Selfridges store

Two ancient universities: Oxford and Cambridge; both of them the pride of England. Oxford! THIS is not Oxford! We had heard that there were not many shops of everyday usage but there were huge shops of books and books alone, as if these people eat books, drink books and dress themselves with books. But here, on Oxford Street, not a hint of books, not a shop or store around. In Oxford town, there should be students and only students and a study-type atmosphere, but in this Oxford Street, there are men in suits, ladies with lipstick and powder and high heels – all of them seem to be very well-dressed. In Oxford, I had heard of the big parks on the banks of the river but here I see no Jehlam, no Satluj-Beas or Ravi-Chinab (the five rivers of the Pinjab). We had heard of the city from the poet Matthew Arnold – "That sweet city with her dreaming spires" – but this architecture is not like that! Here, every building has its own individuality, not a sign of similarity.

Oh yes, the Oxford Street of London is nothing like the famous University city. Oxford is about 50 miles from London and about an hour's drive by car. The one and a half miles of Oxford Street, which is as straight as an arrow, did in fact lead to the city of Oxford. It looks as if the Romans may have built it because it was they who built straight roads. The Romans, for their convenience in Britain, built a straight road from Hampshire to the coast of Suffolk. What is the Oxford Street of

University of Oxford

London? Only one and a half mile stretch of that long road.

At times, other names were given to this part of London. It was once Acton Road, because it goes to Acton. Because it also flows parallel to the Tyburn river, it was at one time named Tyburn Road. It seems Oxford Street owes its name to Lord Oxford. Edward Harley was Earl of Oxford in 1713 and bought the whole of this area of land in one go. This is the reason why some of the streets around Oxford Street are named after his wife or family members. Lord William Bentinck, who was Governor General of India at the time of the infamous famines, was Lord Oxford's elder son-in-law. Because the whole of this estate belonged to one family, it was named as Oxford Street.

The Oxford Street of London is not a tiny Bhairon, Anarkali, Chorra Bazar or Sector 17 of Chandigarh. This is the centre of London, the pride of the capital and also one of the most colourful parts of the city. The pride of this centre, a 400ft (121metres) high 34-storey building was built in 1976 and was named "Centre Point". For a number of years, however, this building remained vacant. Not a candle was lit for a decade. There was no question of the then famous Beatles singing there. Not even the hoot of an owl was heard. However, recently the Department of Trade and Industry decided to locate some of their offices there and now this white elephant of a building is lit beautifully. Designed like a missile, Centre Point occupies only a small area but it does make everybody realise that this is Oxford Street. Not only that, it is now a listed building, which means it cannot be demolished and its continued presence is ensured.

People say that the city of Rome was not built in a day but joke that Chandigarh or Islamabad was built in half a day. That cannot be true. Good things take shape slowly and fruit acquires honey if it ripens slowly.

Oxford Street came into being in the 18th Century with a small gardener's shop and then slowly others started to move in. Drapers came first, then the furniture people and then the cobblers took their benches there. Even today, if you look carefully, there are many shoe stores in this biggest bazaar of London. There may be only one or two booksellers but there are plenty of shoe shops. Even today they entice customers by saying "Buy one pair, get another at half price."

Court proceedings in England years ago were like present day India. A property case would start and would linger on for years before a decision was made on a piece of land. For example, a grandfather who was a fruit merchant, bought a piece of land in the beginning of the 20th Century and his grandson finally got its freehold in 1932. In order to maintain their right of ownership, his father and grandfather always slept on that piece of land. One of the travellers in the beginning of the 18th Century wrote about Oxford Street: "There were houses only at intervals, in this deep, boring and muddy street, where only low and mean grade traders traded."

This most famous bazaar, which started in the 18th Century, carried on making progress even in the 19th Century and, despite some setbacks, became very famous throughout the world. As a result, affluent businessmen from all over the world focused their attention on London because it was the only place in the world where they could get customers in abundance.

Today, the most well known music stores are in Oxford Street. His Master's Voice (HMV) with their famous dog logo, came here as early as 1909 and are known throughout the world. The street is also home to the Virgin music stores. It would be a familiar sight for the young to stand there arm in arm with their friends waiting for hours in order to buy a newly-released CD or album.

World-famous stores like John Lewis, House of Fraser, Selfridge's and Jaeger are here and many date back to 1909.

From the densely populated city of Leeds, Marks and Spencer came to Oxford Street in 1912, and their store there became their most famous. This was evidenced by M&S one year making a £150,000 charity donation to the city council. At their Marble Arch store, they make £1m every hour. There are also three C & A stores alone in this street.

One of the most significant arrivals in Oxford Street was Harry Gordon Selfridge who came over from Chicago in 1905. The American influence on the store he built is quite clear. This single store, now known as Selfridges, once spent about £60m on the renovation of its huge building.

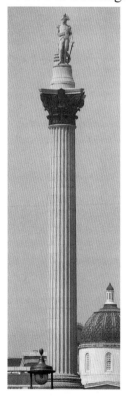

Lord Nelson

In modern times, Britain has created a number of new traditions and pioneered many projects. Like Nelson in wartime, businesses have shown individuality in many fields. When Mr Palmer of London Bridge came into Oxford Street, he fixed the prices of everything in his shop. Other merchants protested and opposed him strongly but he remained firm in his stand. Now, this not only established in Britain but is also slowly prevailing in every corner of the world.

Window display systems were also pioneered by the same Mr Palmer. He displayed everything neatly and in an attractive way. He displayed even loose fabrics by stretching them on boards. Today many people come to Oxford Street just to see these window displays. Tourists can just enjoy looking at the windows and it's all free of charge. The complete honesty of business is what keeps attracting a large number of customers.

Daniel Defoe, known as the first English novelist, also gave some very good suggestions to the traders. For example, the blood should never be visible to the customers and the traders should never create wrinkles on their faces in distaste. Credit was also arranged for the customers and also deliveries.

This bazaar, which developed slowly, can today be described, with much justification, as the most beautiful shopping centre in the world. This is a place where people of all colours, races and who speak over two thousand different languages come together for shopping.

This is a large-sized Anarkali or Palakya bazaar, where rich oil magnates and Arabs flock for shopping. In 1995 Charlotte of Marble Arch, the furniture store, did a sale of £400,000 in two minutes and the eccentric king of Qatar, went out of the shop after "leaving only its

Mrs Gandhi, ex-Prime Minister of India, on a visit to Selfridges.

On V-Day, 8th June 1945. Victory was celebrated with a grand military parade headed by the Royal family, along Oxford Street.

floorboards". London's aim is that every day it should become better and that has been the city's philosophy for the last 200 years. God willing, it will continue.

All the new lines of the best-known British brands are first presented in Oxford Street. If they become popular there they are introduced into the stores in other cities. Whether it be new perfumery, or lingerie-bikini, it comes to Oxford Street first. Only afterwards does it go onward to Birmingham or Glasgow by which time Oxford Street is again getting ready for the new models.

Geographically, Britain may be small in size but the shopping malls of London, in general, and Oxford Street, in particular, are not so small.

Size depends upon the means and imagination of the man. By using the cellars of four or five-storeyed buildings, the space available becomes even more considerable. By using glass, music and screens the general impression of magnitude increases. The welcoming screen of Top Shop superstore is huge and musical performances are continuous. Customers are automatically attracted to the store. The idlers just keep listening to the performances and music, but even the idlers have their value as they indicate that something interesting is happening. Those who come to buy do not hesitate either to spend money.

After selling his business in Chicago, Gordon Selfridge, along with his excellent talent and imagination, arrived in 1905. His solid brick building covers 45,000 square feet. At Selfridges a family can easily spend a day and go home in the evening quite satisfied. I can't say for sure but the simple store could be larger than the whole of Bhairon, Anarkaly, Chorra Bazaar or the sector 17 of Chandigarh. Similarly, the size of Marks and Spencer could be the equivalent of our secretariat and the work force even bigger. West One Shopping Centre, near Bond Street, and the nearby glittering glass building of Burtons reflect pride and business sense.

As soon as people come out of the Underground, this store attracts them immediately. Artists who perform in public also have their eyes on the coins given by passing customers, exactly like our religious singers who always keep their eyes on the charity coins given by the affluent people After seeing everything the store sells, the customers may join the river of people in Oxford Street and perhaps give a few coins to the buskers who are a feature there.

Oxford Street is not very expensive either. Higher prices may well be found in Covent Garden or Sloane Street and the aristocrats and Americans are bound to enjoy a few dramatic performances and an

Anarkaly-type Sunday stroll. Such people may not bother too much about price tags. However, in Oxford Street people are more pragmatic. Everybody knows that this one-and-a-half-mile stretch of London is visited by all types of people and the flood of visitors enhances their sales. Then why loot them? Well-to-do youths first buy their jeans here and then sit in McDonald's and eat together.

You cannot expand and look after businesses unless you have fast means of transport and communication. In this respect, the British are most far-sighted. An illustration of this is the Underground. If people could come only on foot or by car, then not many would come to Oxford Street. A network of underground railways, begun in 1857, runs throughout London. There are no fewer than four rail stops for the one-and-a-half-mile Oxford Street, More than 10 million people make use of these railway stations and people who come out of these stations look like Akalies, the Punjabi political party, going on freedom marches. It looks as if there is a spring of human beings in the ground or as if there is a water pipe in the fields.

For the ten million people of London, there is 63km of line available under the ground, in comparison with Frankfort, which has only 22km, Berlin 39km and Paris, 51km. Not only that, there are 495 bus routes in London while there are only 298 in Paris. Heathrow airport is also the biggest in terms of international passengers, yet it covers only four or five square miles. King Khalid in Saudi Arabia is 81 square miles and Denver International is 52 square miles. It should be remembered that today an aeroplane lands every one and a half minutes.

Thanks are due to the engineers who dug tunnels and started a Chunnel train between Europe and the U.K. Brussels in now only about three hours away from London. In 1996, sea ferries were selling a return ticket to France for just a pound or so. The Government is next thinking of using the Thames for large-scale passenger transport. Boat travel will increase so that the river will be active day and night. Now you ask, should not Oxford Street be like a flooded Jhajjar river?

Unlike other parts of England, pubs and clubs are not immediately visible but they are there if you know where to look. As real estate is too expensive, they are mostly in the cellars of the buildings. The low rent and darker atmosphere suits this trade as well. At 120 Oxford Street, there is the Plaza Shopping Centre, home to the Holmes Place health club. Many visitors from other parts of the world long to see the beautiful blondes who work in the clubs but many of them go back without having a glimpse of them. They should look inside these health clubs. As soon as you enter, you will feel the presence of somebody behind you, most likely a masseuse. Young men and women can take a sauna, swim in the deep pools or just have a massage.

Hit by severe unemployment or by illegal immigration, these will be the girls made recently redundant from the performing arts. Lady Diana spoke up for these girls. Many night clubs sell drinks at half price from 5 to 8pm. You can enjoy the bright

HRH Princess Diana (1961-1997)

lights and the night music. Most interesting time is from 10pm to 1am. Buses run all night in Oxford Street.

Linguists in Punjabi have not been able to earn much of a living in teaching but teachers in English are making gold by being in Oxford Street. There are many English-teaching schools based there which claim to be able to make you fluent in a short span of time.

There is also a church in Oxford Street, St Giles in the Fields. David Garrick, the famous Shakespearean actor got married in this church. The children of poets Shelley and Byron were also baptised here. Even the notorious plague of London took its start from this church in 1665.

The cleanliness and discipline of Oxford Street is also worth noting. Nobody takes paan (similar to chewing tobacco) here but people do have the bad habit of spitting out chewing gum on the footpaths where it sticks like glue. Street sweepers are fighting a never-ending battle with this problem. Most of the stores have such excellent cleanliness in the restrooms that anybody could eat their sandwiches there. A full-time attendant always keeps cleaning them and he does not eat his lunch anywhere else.

It's only buses or taxis (not cars) that run along most of Oxford Street. Nobody can take their two or four-wheeler cars in this street apart from the Queen or the police. Few fights occur and though there is a flood of people, nobody worries about getting their pockets picked or ladies getting annoyed by vagabonds. There are a few people without scruples but not many.

The warning is "There are people selling spurious items" or, in other words "Caveat emptor" which means "Buyer beware.," There is an auction room at numbers 133-135, Oxford Street, whose selling point is that it is all tax-free. Further on Lorenbay representatives had got laryngitis by constant shouting "A bottle of perfume for £10, three for

£20." A woman walking on the footpath might say "As long as the police don't catch me, make the best use of me." Nowhere in the world is so much perfume sold.

Westminster City Council or the Oxford Street Association, if they are in fact there, could stop them. A certain amount of tolerance is part of British culture, a characteristic of the nation who once ruled the waves.

At times you can come across beggars as well. They do not ask you for a full pound, but beg for your change. You can even see somebody in winter using a blanket as they sit on the footpath like a frog or a tortoise. However, you do not often see robberies and this street can get boring as well. So, if possible, enjoy it only a bit at a time.

It is not that accidents don't take place in London, but not many as compared with the rest of the world. It was in 1959 that a man died after an electric lamp fell on him. Also at the same place in the same year when another man died after a 15 foot electric pole fell down on him. The *Evening Standard* newspaper created such a hue and cry that London became very angry.

Before Christmas, London is lit up in December to attract customers to the shops and visitors to the city. This ceremony of switching on the lights is done each year by a dignitary or celebrity.

Regent Street in Piccadilly pioneered this tradition in 1954, then others followed. Oxford Street has done so since 1959. When Prince Charles became 30 in 1978, Oxford Street gave him this honour. Britain fought a successful war with Falklands in 1982 where Prince Andrew piloted a helicopter. After the victory, he was asked to switch on the lights. In 1981, the beauty queen, Miss Universe, was from England so she did the switching-on. In 1985, Bob Geldof collected huge sums of money for charity and he was given the privilege. So it goes on.

Some of the top business people get together in Oxford Street for the annual ceremony. The man or woman of the moment then comes out of a store to be greeted by applause, goes on a high vehicle and switches on the lights. "Let there be light" he or she says, with his hands together. The street gets lit. People go to their homes but the hero or heroine is famous as well as affluent.

Theft is always a headache in business, whether it be employee theft or, more likely, shop-lifting by outsiders. In business language, it is called "shrinkage". It is estimated that there is shrinkage of about £1,000m in the whole of British shops or stores. The big stores of Oxford Street have had their own personal guards since the beginning of the 20th Century but despite that they lose £100m every year. This is called a "golden mile" in robbers' terminology. Half of the burglary is done with bank credit cards and the other £50m worth of goods are simply taken. It is not ordinary housewives who steal the expensive smoked salmon but well-organised burglars, some perhaps even dressed in police uniforms. At one time, "bloomers" were in fashion in England and these could be used as a type of gunny sack to smuggle valuable goods out of a store.

Perfumery, lipsticks, silky clothes, or Parker pens were among the favourite items of these conniving women. By hiding them in their bloomers, they would sing mischievous songs such as "Bloomers have manifold advantages, we just slip these things in like a dive." Modern-day thieves when caught begin trembling but locals are fast enough to run.

The police now have fixed surveillance cameras everywhere. Only about 10,000 thieves ever go to the courts, although there are many more who get caught. One can imagine the amount of sales in Oxford Street from their shrinkage alone. Five billion pounds is earned every year from an area of five million square feet and by only 300 hoteliers or shopkeepers.

Bogus protests or empty patriotic slogans do not make a nation. They are built by putting your head on your palm and by getting cut like mince meat. Oxford Street does not forget their heroic patriots who laid down their lives during the two world wars. About two million British were killed and many others were wounded in the First World War. This loss of life is still commemorated every year and those from Oxford Street stores who laid down their lives have their names engraved on the beautiful ornamented plates hung in the shops. In many cases, those who were injured in the wars were retrained and taken back to do other jobs.

The First World War ended on November 11, 1918, at 11am. One of the most famous Oxford Street stores would have a bugle played on that day every year at 11 o'clock. As soon as the Last Post was played, everybody would stop what they were doing. People would doff their hats and pay homage to the martyrs. When the bugle changed its tune to *Reveille*, they would walk away after putting their wet handkerchiefs in their pockets. This homage to the martyrs carried on for decades, every year up to the end of the Second World War when Selfridges was the superstore that carried on the tradition.

Gordon Selfridge (1864-1947), the founder of Selfridges.

World-famous facia of Selfridges in Oxford Street.

A most interesting point to note is that the owner of this store, Gordon Selfridge, was a non-British foreigner, who with the cooperation of the indigenous people, achieved great heights in business. Everybody always looks with respect at the brass plate which commemorates him.

The expressions of happiness are worth noticing when tourist buses roar into Oxford Street. The scene is one of smiling children, old men clapping, dancing, hooting whistling and flanking mufflers.

"Hey, hey" cry the people walking on the footpaths and they lift their arms in happiness.

Every new day, every minute, all 12 months of the year, it looks as if both the parties are saying "Merry Christmas" or "Happy New Year" to each other.

Written in 1997

A Punjabi Poet in London -
My Personal Journey

At the end of the sixties, black and brown people in Britain were a bit shaken, after a Wolverhampton MP, Enoch Powell, delivered a speech accusing them of being the potential cause of looting, riots and bloodshed in the future. The infamous speech, commonly known as the "River of Blood" speech, had the opposite result to what Powell intended and expected. In fact, it was instrumental in getting minorities organised under the guidance, in Wolverhampton, of Aaron Haynes, a black graduate born in America. At that time, we Punjabis were newcomers in this society but Aaron was one who was forged in the States in a multi-cultural, multi-racial society. His statements were always an answer to Powell's rhetoric. It should be remembered that it was about this time that Martin Luther King was shot dead.

Niranjan Singh Noor (1933-1999) (left) and Enoch Powell MP (1912-1998).

From left: Aaron Haynes, Community Relations Officer Wolverhampton; Martin Luther King (1929-1968) and Hardev Dhesi (1933-1998).

Among the locals who led opposition to Powell's views were Dr Frank Reeves, Italian-born Dr Barnsby and Dr Wymer (who later became the principal of Bilston Community College) and among the Asians, Hardev Singh Dhesi, Professor Surjit Singh Khalsa and myself.

With the sudden deaths of Naranjan Singh Noor (1937–1998) and Hardev Singh Dhesi (1933–1998), in a short span of six weeks, it looked as if the curtains were closing on the first generation of immigrants into Britain. As well as being necessary to pay tribute to Noor the Punjabi

Left: Cedric Taylor, Chairman of Birmingham's Standing Conference of West Indian Organisation. Middle: Eric Irons, a Jamaican who became Britain's first coloured magistrate. Right: Dr Doojen Napal, former exiled member of the Mauritian Parliament, edited the West Midlands' only multi-lingual newspaper 'Pardesi'. This writer and Dr Napal were big supporters of integration and our magazine's emblem showed a white hand grasping a black hand in friendship.

poet, it also behoves Wulfrunians to commemorate Hardev, who spent his first few years in Wolverhampton.

Whether in Wolverhampton or London, Hardev Dhesi and Naranjan Noor joined hands in serving the community. Both were teachers, who came to England in the flood of immigration in 1962. They did teacher training in the same year at Wolverhampton. Hardev died a mere six weeks before Noor.

Here we can briefly evaluate the contributions of two contemporary practical men in theory and practice.

In their careers in England, Hardev was the pathfinder of Noor and had attained a much higher standard of living than Noor had. Noor was a father of four but Hardev was without children. He was virtually a hermit. Noor became interested in buying property and did so many times, here as well as back in India. Hardev never regretted not having children.

Today, when we hear the songs or poems of Noor, we can also hear an echo of Hardev's persuasive voice – a voice that emerged through his shaved and cut moustache, giving him a westernised appearance in Wolverhampton.

Hardev was able to win each and everybody's friendship, while Noor at times could lose the support of people who mattered. Hardev was like the branch of a toot tree – similar to the willow – with loose and flexible branches. Noor, however, was stubborn like an elephant's trunk. Hardev could overlook or forget certain matters, while Noor would carry on chewing the same venom over and over again. Sweet-spoken was our Hardev but Noor, while outwardly appearing to be sweet, could do his share of back-stabbing. Hardev was fearless as well as being without ill-will. At times Noor was also fearless but he had a substantial list of enemies and opponents. Most of those who chose to oppose him tended to be illiterate people who would talk about him only over a drink in pubs, but would not communicate his misdeeds overseas.

Many of Noor's opponents appeared in numbers to pay their last homage to him. Surprisingly, though, one of his colleagues who once lived in Walsall, then in Birmingham and Coventry, did not attend his funeral. However, a linguist and scholar, who once claimed in a Conservative manifesto that the post-graduate Punjabi class run by Noor at Bilston College was an insult to Punjabi universities, did attend – and he walked about two miles to do so. When asked why, he replied: "We should take care of some of the good characteristics of our culture. No need to rejoice when an enemy dies, because you will die as well."

What we are now noticing in Wolverhampton, after 35 years, is that people from around 35-mile radius are coming here to enjoy the night life. There may be workers strikes at certain places, but definitely there is no fight between the black and white people.

Wolverhampton Council for Community Relations, referred to

Left: Dr Dhani Prem, an Indian, Deputy Chairman of the Commonwealth Welfare Council and Birmingham Councillor. He suggested local immigrants put up General Election candidates. Middle: Hamza Alavi, Pakistani writer, Vice-Chairman of CARD. He saw integration coming - "perhaps in two generations time." Right: Dr David Pitt, a West Indian who chaired the 'Campaign Against Racial Discrimination' and became the first Negro to stand for Parliament.

earlier, was set up in our city to combat racism. In order to uplift our spirits, Hardev Dhesi put before us the example of Lala Hardyal – the freedom fighter of India – that a person who wants to serve his country and make money at the same time is nothing but a whore.

Hardev had the same courage and spirit of the Indian freedom fighters, such as Gadri Babe, but Noor, on the other hand, would also carry on counting on his fingers, as if counting his money, even while reciting his poems.

Hardev was an ascetic and his main characteristic was that of a sincere hermit. Our Noor completed his life span by swaying to both sides. One of our nearest and dearest critics, who is well known in the capitals, on his visit to England, could not even sense this side of Noor which resulted in his judgement being a bit one-sided.

Hardev was miles away from hypocrisy. The years that he spent in our city as a clean-shaven man were cheerful. Then when he went to London and well before 1984 – the year of the Amritsar tragedy – he converted himself to a proper Sikh with a turban and beard and he stuck to that for life. Our Noor, on the other hand, mostly shaved with razor but at times with scissors. For example, he would put on a turban and trim his beard, but at other times would not. He would go without a turban to see George Fernandis but with a colourful turban when to see Bhindranwale. "A Ganga Ram, when he visits Ganges and Jumna Dass, when going to the Jumna river,"– can these be the characteristics of an ascetic? Whenever people go on a protest march, they would look forward like soldiers. Noor would pick the flag up like others but would carry on looking back most of the time. If you are protesting, it should be like Master Tara Singh, so that if ever the call comes, you should be able to cut off your opponents.

Noor's tongue was always ready to make fun of a lady sex-writer living in England. No reasonable gentleman with a dynamic personality would ever do this mean act but Hardev deserves credit even in this respect.

If others would wear out their shoes or tyres in six months, Noor's would last only three. There were two reasons for that – he was a tireless worker but did not drive a car. Poetry was his vehicle. He used his poetry to become a leader and when after the 'turban case' he managed to collect some funds, it was because of his poems.

It cannot be emphasised too greatly just how much he helped others. He spent many hours serving his community.

In one respect, there is a similarity between Noor and Harbhajan Yogi of America. When Yogi went to the States, his friends advised him that you cannot do without a car there. Yogi in turn replied in full

Harbhajan Virk addressing a few Punjabi writers in Wolverhampton (organised by Progressive Writers Association).

confidence saying: "He does not need a car who is in tune with One God (Ek Onkar)." People would run after Yogi to listen to his lectures.

Contrary to that, Noor did try to learn how to drive but failed every time, a total of nine in all. A volcano of poetry was erupting out of him and so people themselves would give him a lift. Noor was the only Punjabi poet living in England who managed to get plenty of lifts through his poetry.

A literary man is a creative writer and not a car driver. Anybody could drive Dodi or Diana's car but only the chosen few can write *From Harappa to Hiroshima* or *Heer* of Waris Shah.

When doctors suggested to Noor that his time on earth was limited, he snatched and used the literary writing of his best friend Harbhajan Virk, who collected them after years of hard work in his book *Exiled Punjab*. Harbhajan always drove for Noor, but in turn Noor used almost all the material of his *Healthy Living Punjab*. Shedding real tears, Virk

Dr Harbhajan Singh from Delhi University on the right, Cllr. Mota Singh ex-Mayor of Leamington Spa on the left and Noor addressing the writers.

felt he was "slain by his own friend", who he felt had plagiarised his work and would show his writings to his friend, as Guru Arjun showed to Mian Mir. Virk was very remorseful over this act of betrayal.

A successful director is he who would guide his organisation by limiting his expenses. He is the head of his organisation and his employees are his legs and arms. The director has to keep an eye on them, lead them and if necessary reprimand them as well. The directors of Bilston Community College could not achieve that, which I believe contributed to its bankruptcy. This was the college, where Noor ran his MA Punjabi course and was proud of doing so. By showing a deficit of £4m, the college, which was devoted to the community, lost its existence. Noor was one of those responsible and many of the Punjabi language teachers lost their jobs. There was much publicity about this in our local newspaper, *Express & Star*, alleging misuse of funds at the college.

In order to appreciate and evaluate Noor's other contributions, it is necessary to recall how and when the Asian immigrants came to Britain.

Unlike America, Canada or Australia, the top Indian talent never came to Britain. The overall impression of the Indian community living in the United States is that they are well-educated people, and are either doctors or engineers. However, it has never been so in Britain though no doubt in the Sixties a few teachers or skilled workers did immigrate.

The Immigration Act of 1962 applied mostly to ex-servicemen and due to the dire need for manpower after the Second World War, they were recruited in haste. They were very hardworking but did not know English. Now retired, they were Noor supporters, and were essentially "yes" men.

Whether the concert-conference was in Bilston College or anywhere else, like recruits they went where they were told. And see, what else?

Mr and Mrs Puri, Assistant High Commissioner of India, the writer Manmohan Maheru, the Mayor of Wolverhampton Cllr. Tony Guy and Cllr. Shadi Sharma on the right in the Wolverhampton Civic Hall in the sixties.

They must clap like monkeys when they see others clap. Apart from the chief guest from India or a few scattered poets from other nearby towns, the majority of the audience were these puppet clappers. The audience, even though they were not white-collared clerks, solicitors or teachers, were definitely mesmerised. In the evening whenever they were relaxing on Banks's beer in the Lewisham Arms pub, after working 10 or 12 hours in factories and fire-lit foundries, Noor would often read his poetry.

This was the type of audience who were impressed most by Noor. He tried to help them relax either by singing or reading from *Mukti*. When he could not make his mark as a politician and his colleagues asked for the accounts of the Turban Action collections, Noor left them in the lurch and turned his attention to poetry alone. That is why his production was comparatively greater in his final years.

A critic's job is not to receive adulation from his audience but to evaluate what the artist says and what he actually does. He should also look into the artist's misdeeds or mean activities as a man or a leader. To be hailed by the applause of such an audience is not the criterion for evaluating a poet – this is our firm belief. We also do not consider it a pious act when the book Noor's Wanjara was compiled by asking many people to write about him.

At times, when Noor delivered a speech, it was emotionally charged and not appealing so much to the head. At times it was also a bit rude. You need a refined and civilised language, because you are living in a most civilised democracy.

After Sardul of Southall, 25-year-old Shadi Sharma of Wolverhampton was elected the second Labour councillor in Britain in 1973. He was a very promising boy, who today could easily have been the Prime Minister, and this writer was his inspirer. I galvanised him by telling him the stories of patriots and freedom fighters of India. When a death occurred in his garment factory, Noor accused him in such a way that Sharma went back to Delhi and set up in business there.

Noor often used accusatory language long before Enoch Powell's "River of

Shadi Sharma, second Asian Labour Cllr. elected in 1973. He raised a voice for city status of Wolverhampton.

blood" speech and occasionally got into trouble because of it, whether it be directed towards Margaret Thatcher or Indira Gandhi. For example, the expression "tail of the dog" was used for Enoch and "Hitler's sister" for Indira.

Linguists term it alliteration, when adjacent sounds begin with the same letter. "Wailing in the winter wind" is an example. Because it has an emotional touch, such a style looks interesting but it does not necessarily appeal to the intellect. However, Noor the poet increased the impact of his poems by using such alliterative words.

Some of his friends used Noor for their own interests. They were his friends, of course, but whenever they had the chance, they would backstab Noor, by using alliterative language facetiously, such as, "He was a good poet but not a good politician. It was our protest about wearing a turban and the question of our self respect, but the poet has misused it."

The Common Market allocated quite a bit of money to the Bilston College to teach the Punjabi language there. Everyone was happy since it might motivate our second generation to learn their mother tongue. However, in collaboration with the Punjabi University, they started teaching BA and MA in Punjabi. What did Noor achieve by conferring MA degrees on three or four persons only? They already knew Punjabi quite well. The goal should have been to create immense interest in the new generation's children. Thus, language could lead to Punjabi literature and literature in turn could give them the sense and the colour of Punjabi culture for a long time.

To institute a dispute with a British headmaster in the "turban case" was simply posturing. England is a very civilised country and the people have always used polite language to each other. We immigrants are lucky in that they recognised us and we know their history quite well.

Unlike Bawa Balwant, Tara Singh or Deepak Jatoi, Noor was quite well off. Sixty thousand pounds was not such a burden to him, which he could not pay and this amount was peanuts for an organisation.

In the eighties, this writer invested about half a million pounds along with his friends and supporters. When somehow the bottom fell out, this writer, under the supervision of the Financial Services Authority, paid back all that to them. Noor, being a friend, also invested quite a bit which was returned to him after getting his signature. It is a matter of principle, of honest commitment of personality and of being a sound person. This is something to think about not a bogus self-appraisal.

> *"The fight is of the people and the bloodsuckers.*
> *The fight has reached its climax.*
> *The fight is between the workers and their exploiters."*

Here we will interpret one of his poems which he generally read at the concerts and for which he received much applause.

"Ajj larai lokan di te jokan (leech) di?"

Dr Sathi Ludhianvi, a writer/radio and TV presenter of London.

Dr Davinder Kaur, a writer and singer of Wolverhampton.

The English translation is *"Who are these people and who the leeches?"* During the last 250 years of industrial revolution, the idlers have seldom been able to make much. Despite that, exploiters have been carrying on their businesses and sometimes they get hit themselves.

"And who are the "blood-suckers?" Social Security has been in place for the last 50 years and a lot of idlers have been nourishing their families on it and also carrying on with their hobbies. Out of the unemployed, there are many of musicians, goldsmiths or literary men who are writing full time. What should we call them? Writers of the people or leeches of society? Out of them, who is Noor's worker? Is he just putting an injection of poetry in order to consolidate his leadership? This could be true of any other country of the world but not of Britain! Then why applaud? What is the philosophy behind it? Or high seriousness?

Guest critics – who are specially invited from India – are unable to understand these minute things. It is not a critic's role or place to get intoxicated by such applause.

In most of Noor's poetry, we do not find the high-seriousness of Baba Farid, not the pace and flow of Amrita, but plenty of "Harippa" of Bhangra folksong.

Let us consider the first poem of Hayati Di Hook:

> "Jang da baddal gajjda Jikoon,
> Wajda jiwain duggara,
> Dozakh di bhatti ton amian,
> Dozakh da bhai mara."

Punjabi folk singer Malkit Singh MBE.

79

Cllr. Ranjit Dheer (Ex-Mayor of Ealing) and Varinder Sharma MP Ealing, London.

Noor seems to have read Mohan Singh Mahir's Savain Patter before he wrote his *Mukti*. The influence of Sheikh Sadi and Guru Gobind Singh seems to be prevailing in *Ho Chi Minh*.

In order to reflect her devotion and indebtedness, the song *Diva bal ke rakhin* that Dr Davinder Kaur often sings in poetical symposiums is really a good song, a song that embodies optimism in life.

A life-long literary conflict carried on between Dr Chanan Singh Chan and Noor. We strongly recommend enthusiastic readers to go through and analyse critically the parodies written by Chanan and published in *Des Pardes Weekly*.

Principal Sukhjinder Sangha of Lichfield, a voluminous writer.

As Punjab has not been able to produce a hero after King Porus, who fought against Alexander the Great, similarly no leader has yet been accepted in the UK. Whenever the minority communities face extreme injustice and atrocities, the true hero – in word and deed – will come forth automatically. It will not happen before that. This is our belief. Vishnu Datt and Jagmohan Joshi did have

Inderjit Singh Sangha, Dr C. S. Chann, Dr R. Reehal, and Teja Singh Tej.

the potential, but even the literary societies forget Noor's memory.

The art of poetry can not be separated from the man. Poetry does not give birth to the man, this is the totality of the man, it is his voice, his pains and pangs and the wailing cries of his soul. Poetry that emits fragrance cannot flow out of a rotten man. This is not only Noor's legacy, this is the character of many poets.

"If you want to catch a thief, send a thief" is an Irish saying. In a similar manner anybody who has seen Noor's lifestyle for the last half a century can analyse him minutely. Guest speakers invited from overseas cannot help taking sides.

Punjabi the language will be better served if Noor is evaluated in the context of the immigrant country like Dulla Bhatti in King Akbar's time. There are many other worthy poets to be considered.

Friends, let there be not just false appraisal, like Atam Hamrahi's *Dhrutara* or Malkiat's *Tootak Tootak Tutian*. We do not want to hit below the belt either, but to find the real gist after discarding the written word around it. We, the writers in Britain, will be blamed afterwards, if we do not say the truth now.

> "Jadon tak tare kehan te,
> Karan de wich farak hei,
> Toon frebi hain te,
> Teri kala kumbhi narak hai."

Then you yourself decide, my friends:

> "Kiwain bakshe jange,
> Jo punn de na te gunah kite gaye."

Writing an essay is not the art of a novel. There are limitations. I can send the addresses of the following, who would like to dig deeper!

1. Giani Reshan Singh – President N.R.I. Sabha Jalandher.
2. Dr Rattan Reehal – author of thirty books in Punjabi.
3. Harbhajan Virk – Noor's chariotman, friend, publisher
4. Aug-Sep 1999 *Meri Boli Mare Dharam* magazine
5. Shadi Sharma – the second Labour councillor in Britain.
6. Naranjan Dhillon – Head, Khalsa College, Sedgley Street, Wolverhampton
7. Avtar Uppal – singer, musician, leader, London
8. Councillor Mota Singh – ex mayor, Leamington Spa
9. Prof Surjit Khalsa – full report and pamphlets of turban committees
10. Dish Judge – ex general secretary, Indian Workers' Association

11. Sarwan Singh Leamington – the right hand of Jagmohan Joshi
12. Mohan Maheli – ex general secretary Indian Workers' Association
13. Sarwan Bharat – ex general secretary Indian Workers' Association
14. Avtar Sadaq – Leicester, writer, leader, European leader Surjit
15. Comrade Sarwan Singh – Harkishan Singh Surjit's disciple
16. Ajmer Coventry – Leader, writer
17. Dr Bhardwaj – a linguist, ex lecturer at Bilston College
18. Harbaksh Maksudpuri – writer, critic
19. Surjan Duhra – ex mayor, Wolverhampton
20. And many more that you can find with your gift of polite tongue

Written in 2006

The Development of Birmingham Asians' Business Group

Selfridges store, Bull Ring, Birmingham.

When I was a student in India, Britain was the unobtainable idealistic dream – the land of milk and honey, the land of poets and prophets, of sages and seers, and. above all, of beauty and freedom. In addition to bettering ourselves financially, the burning passion was also to see the Shakespearean theatres and Hardy's landscapes. There is no doubt that if we go a few miles out, we see the flowers, the gentle hills and the green downs. We are really carried away with delight. The weather may not be good but the people are kind, young ladies are very nice and Yorkshire pudding is the best dish in the world. There is also a tremendous sense of safety and freedom here. These are the things you do not appreciate unless you have lived without them.

Britain is, perhaps the only country in the world which has all opportunities for all human beings equally, and all facilities to educate oneself. There are chances for men to stand on their own two feet. Administration over here is quite neat and tidy. In Asia, he still feels that he was "born

Sir James Watts (1736-1819) of Industrial Revolution.

Council House, Birmingham

free and is everywhere in chains."

The harsh realities of life are that nobody can flee from his own country's history and few people ever escape the consequences of the past. The sins of the fathers do indeed descend on the third or even the fourth generations.

The community, as has been pointed out by Burke, is born of a historical partnership of the living, the dead and the unborn. Let us trace a bit of the Asian history. To start with, about 2,000 years ago, Diodorus spoke of India in glowing terms. He found India a large, well-watered, fertile land where two crops were harvested each year. In the first century BC, India was so prosperous that Diodorus could write, "This is the reason, they say, why a famine has never visited India, there never being any lack of food among them."

All through the centuries, this prosperity continued. Then came the period when Moguls started their rule. India was very prosperous during those days and was no doubt termed "a golden sparrow". Her wealth and prosperity attracted foreign businesses, including the British East India Company.

Lord William Bentinck (1774-1839), Governor General Of India from 1833-1835.

On this side, thanks are due to the people of the Black Country who sacrificed a lot and did wonders in inventing machines. Machines created leisure and this resulted in the progress of world civilisations.

On the other hand, on the

continent of Asia, with the Battle of Plessey in 1757, the British rule in India began with outright plunder. The land revenue imposed by the British authorities extracted the uttermost farthing, not only from the living but also from the dead cultivators. Clive, the empire builder, was largely responsible for this pure loot. Later on this loot was called 'trade' and 'trade' was plunder. There are few instances in history of anything like that and this lasted under various names and under different forms, not for a few years but for centuries.

All this resulted in the famous famines of India. The series of films recently shown about India reflect a period of stress and strain for Britain. The working class became unemployed. They died in tens of millions. It is not a false statement but an historical fact which neither *The Far Pavilions* nor *The Jewel in the Crown* has touched upon at all. I still remember the lines of history when Governor General Lord William Bentinck reported in 1854 that the misery hardly finds a parallel in the history of commerce. "The bones of cotton weavers are bleaching the plains of India." India can therefore take pride in the fact that she helped greatly in giving birth to

In the seventies, Asians on their way to Britain waiting in the airport lounge in Nairobi. Fears that Kenya's new Immigration Bill will make Asians into second class citizens are behind the exodus.

the Industrial Revolution. Begun in the year 1770, 13 years after Plessey was fought.

This was followed by rigorous attempts to restrict and crush Indian manufacturers by various means and internal duties. The original Indian textile industry collapsed and Lancashire, with English manufacturing capabilities, became the new centre of the Indian textile industry. The raw cotton was grown in India; cloth was manufactured in England and then sold back to India. This policy continued throughout the 19th Century, breaking up old industries – ship-building, metal-working, glass, paper and many crafts. Just imagine what course a man will take under such circumstances.

Freedom is a divine thing, but freedom to die of starvation is not so divine. Under such adverse circumstances, our hero leaves India and looks for work in the continent of Africa. He works hard in the fields and later on he helps the British in the construction of railways and other projects in Africa. In one of his novels, *Green Hills of Africa*, the honest novelist Hemingway says on page 273 "It took an Indian to make money from sisal and on the coast every coconut plantation meant a man ruined by the idea of making money from cobra."

Moreover, due to changing historical circumstances, we find that in country after country – in Africa and in Asia – Indians being treated as unwanted people and being sent out with very little of their savings made during many years of their labour, enterprise and careful living during their sojourn in these lands. Burma evicted some of the writer's family, impounding – or stealing more like – their belongings in the form of land and money. These memories are still fresh in our minds, Powerless, toothless and clawless, our hero lost his property many a time.

Britain being the mother country of the Commonwealth, an Asian immigrant has full faith in the system. This being one of the most civilised countries of the world, an Asian businessman feels confidence in the administration. The British are the most level-headed people in the world. History is witness to that. Revolutions can come in other countries and a few can imitate them but nobody ever felt the need for such drastic changes over here. If justice is ever done in the world, it is done in Britain. It is this faith in the grandeur of British character which gives so much of the incentive to Asian businessmen to work, invest and re-invest in this country. We know that Britain will never betray the trust and will never turn their immigrants out with bag and baggage. No other country in the world can be trusted with as much confidence as Britain.

Despite the unforgotten negatives often associated with the era of the British Raj in our motherland, it did give us our systems of railway lines, education, laws and the most cherished gift of all, democracy – the freedom of every citizen, regardless of colour, creed, origin or livelihood, to be able to elect their own governance. Corruption put to one side, she is still the largest democracy in the world, thanks in essence to the Raj, with a little help

Poet and Politician Edmund Waller (1606-1687).
"To dig for wealth, we weary not our limbs;
Gold, though the heaviest metal, hitherto swims,
Ours is harvest where the Indians mow,
We plough the deep, and reap what others sow."

Women polling in Rai Bareli Constituency during the fourth General Election in India.

from a tough young man who was given an open opportunity to live and study in India's sister country, Great Britain.

If there had ever been a secret conspiracy to destroy our nation, then would not Mahatma Gandhi have been assassinated long before he was able to remove metaphorical chains and help start the foundation for countless more democracies that were spawned. England made that possible. For that the Indian and African sub-continents are for ever indebted. Had there not been this faltering integrity, sincerity and genuine longing within the framework of the United Kingdom's approach to her past colonisation this could never have been remotely possible. This was their wisdom – the British wisdom.

It almost seems unfashionable in this day and age to sing the praises of a former intruder but life boils down to many inexplicable riddles. It is these riddles that are the DNA, so to speak, of the only thing more important than life itself – naturally, the truth.

Singing praises is one thing but taking an extra paragraph to underscore one of the most historically important feathers that any European country can wear proudly in her cap or crown is nothing short of a simple reciprocation for the honesty and sincerity

Statue of Lady Wulfruna at Civic Square, Wolverhampton.

which England has striven to share and instill in other nations, returning here in simple, humble literary form.

Once, a letter written by a senior African-Indian immigrant appeared in the *Indian Express* and read: "My skin is bruised and scarred by the barbed jibes and taunts directed against me as an Indian." Then he gives a catalogue of opprobrious epithets with which Indians are derided in Burma, Ceylon, Malaysia, Kenya, Zanzibar and East and Central Africa.

An Asian immigrant now feels that economic progress and resurrection is the only way to wash this historical stigma from his face. Hence he works hard in business. This, I feel, is the background turmoil working behind their minds.

Economically, Indian settlers in South Africa and East Africa have always been better off than their relatives in India. Despite apartheid, very few Indian settlers return home because in India they would have to face worse problems than apartheid. Historical factors have contributed to the unfortunate fact that India sits forever on a communal volcano, just as America is always cautious about racial matters.

This time, the stage being Britain, our hero's attempt is again to create a new life in a new country. No-one who is financially secure, politically well connected and socially established emigrates from India. The Asian businessman, therefore, is made of sterner stuff.

He cannot forget the corrupt administration of his mother country. He escapes from a society that denies opportunity, disallows social equality, restricts recognition and crushes fulfillment of natives. He is in Britain primarily to make money. No doubt he has developed the habit of saving a bit and then ploughing it back into his business. In addition, the harder work ethic of the immigrant businessman further divides him from the majority

Women's work, by Rose Garrard, 1997, commemorates working women of the Black Country.

community who are meticulous about holidays and work hours and resent both the infringement and the consequent competition.

"Love thy work" – could there be a better life motto? Vedanta, an ancient Indian book written four thousand years ago, teaches us to work with detachment, irrespective of the result of that work. This is a good spiritual philosophy. In other words, we do not work for results but for human satisfaction and for the health of both body and mind.

Work is among the few things that exist for their own sake. Art for art's sake results in artiness; love for love's sake leads to the divorce court; religion for religion's sake leads to fanaticism.

Our first generation businessman, who actually dared to set up a small business, was not an educated man. He comes from a rural rustic background. To know his background, we had better go with Virgil and say "Come let us go into the fields, let us lodge in the village."

None of them knew much about the structure of commerce and industry in this country. From the very nature of his work, a jeans manufacturer cultivated close intercourse with his machinists. It is the organisation that matters, the day-to-day contact with the customer as well as the labour force. He was quick in making decisions and was a self-supporting all-rounder in the turmoil of his business affairs.

It has been said that after the Fall of Man in the Garden of Eden,

The Elizabeth blast furnace of Bilston Steelworks is on its way down towards the ground. Photo courtesy of Express & Star.

Eve asked Adam what the matter was. Adam simply replied; "Nothing, my dear, we are in a state of transition." The Asian businessman, I should say, is in a state of transition.

Second generation Asians are those born and brought up in Britain, whose only contact with India is through their parents. The enlightened education system of this country has widened the horizons of thinking. They look upon India with the same wonderment and despair as any foreigner. To them, it is exotic, alluring, depressing, disillusioning, dissident and

The writer Manmohan Singh Maheru in the centre, Baldev Singh Aujla on the left and Harbhajan Singh Nijjar on the right. Photo Courtesy of Birmingham Post, March 25, 1982.

perhaps challenging – but it is not home. The country they identify with is Britain.

At the same time, they have not forgotten the sad "sweetest" memories of their fathers who used to work in the Bennids of Smethwick, the Qualcasts of Wolverhampton or the British Steels of Bilston. They feel, with Alexander Pope "We think our fathers fools, so wise we grow. Our natural sons no doubt will think us so."

During this period of transition, we are passing through a sort of cultural revolution. The days of blind faith seem to be over and we have learned to see everything quite critically and rationally. Being settled in a different atmosphere, we have changed our traditional values and attitudes towards life's problems. Propagation of practices which produce nothing has been dropped. The traditional Indian yoga and meditation are forbidden for us. It is for the American and European idlers to imitate the Indian meditation systems. These are for peace of mind, we are told in India. However, peace of mind is a sterile concept which produces nothing but peace of mind. Everything else worthwhile, such as running a business or creating a work of art, is the product of active agitated minds. There is an apt quotation from an Asian poet, Allama Iqbal:

"Khuda tujhey kisi toofan
Sey ashana kar dey,
Ke terey bahar ki maujon
meiztirab nahin"

"May God bring a storm in your life,
there is no tumult in the waves of your life's sea"

We have outlawed practices which have no rational basis or cannot be scientifically proved. Back at home, we the Indians spend – I might even say, waste – an enormous part of our time in prayer, ritual and pilgrimages. You may have smelled a bit of this atmosphere in *The Far Pavilions* and *The Jewel in the Crown* series shown on TV. The revered 'mystics' or 'hermits' of India are no more than 'holy beggars' in our minds. Our ideal is not a secluded saint in saffron robes, but a "Karma Yogi" in a labourer's soiled clothes. Our motto is "Work is worship but

The Repertory Theatre, Birmingham

worship is not work."

In India there is a reverence for the past, for tradition, for custom, for sacred cows and sacred writings. In all that, we the Asians have replaced our reverence for work. "Work is life, life is work" – that is our motto. No doubt, through that we are turning our leisure time into sublimity.

A Punjabi marriage is fairly stable and long lasting. This stability creates faith and faith gives incentive and encouragement for making more and more money. Believe it or not, in our society there is a psychological reaction to the very mention of the word 'divorce'. In this age of reason, we still believe that it is a pious affair. A wife may at times be a burden to others but an Asian wife is an economic treasure for us.

To quote a Multani proverb, "A Jat (peasant) wife for me – all the rest a mere waste of money." Back at home in Asia, our women used to work hard. In addition to cleaning the house and preparing the meals, they used to feed the cattle, churn the milk and above all milk the she-buffaloes two or three times a day. For a woman who used to take the ploughman's food with fodder as head load to distant fields, working 12 hours in a shop or ten hours in a factory is still child's play.

History, said Burke, teaches us not principles but prudence. In respect of their labour relations an Asian

The writer, Manmohan Maheru, and Dave Allcock, the manager, in 'Made in the Black Country' column of Express & Star, 21 March 2003.

businessman is simply using his prudence. He does not consider his workers merely as workers. He tries to keep social and family relations with his workers. The Asian directors usually do not spend their weekends on the coast. They instead attend their workers' marriages or their children's birthday parties. They usually remain at each others' backs. If a worker needs money in an emergency, the employer helps him. On the other hand, if an employer has no money to pay, the workers

can remain patient for a considerable time. Business and labour therefore are not rivals. A director is not a boss in the factory. He is usually addressed as "Brother" or "Comrade".

When a man or woman joins a factory, he or she gives their best to their employer. Employers in turn are as much reluctant to fire them as they are to turn a son out of a family. This father-son loyalty is an important factor in our success.

Our workers have an incomparable dedication

Manmohan Singh, vice-president of the J.W. Hunt Cup, hands over a cheque to Karen Gullick, community fund-raising officer, watched by Nigel Stones, manager of Barclays in Sedgley, assistant manager Jan Smith, Ken Bullock, chairman of the Beacon Centre, and Walter Wakeman, treasurer of the J.W. Hunt Cup on Oct 6, 2011. Photo courtesy of Express & Star and The Chronicle.

to work. It is in the soul and character of our "A" workers to be drawn into their work – to enter into what they are doing with deep penetration. Inspired religious hymns and erotic love songs are sung side by side in the workshops. Men and women work in concentrated silence. The atmosphere is of well-focused energy and disciplined good cheer. Our workers, whenever we need, are ready to stop over. Their attention is always on the task in hand rather than on the clock.

No wonder that an Asian employer can quote competitive prices. The writer of these lines had 20 years' practical experience in this field and is writing as a result of his own bone and blood experience. It has now become an established fact in business circles that the Asian firms are more competitive than the indigenous ones. One of the many reasons is that the production workers put their best in their work. They usually do not smoke and are not habitual tea drinkers.

No wonder the workers are devoted to their work and not to their "leaders" who are all the time agitating for higher wages, better amenities, greater privileges and fewer responsibilities.

Council of Sikh Gurdwaras in Wolverhampton presenting a cheque for £15,000 to the vice-consulate of Pakistan Arif Mahmood for earthquake relief. Around £30,000 was raised from the appeal, with half going to disaster fund and other half going to non-profit organisation called United Sikhs. Photo courtesy of Express & Star.

Let us now see how an Asian starts in business. While children, we used to sing:

"Snow mountains aloft to beckon us, hot plains so wide,
Indus and Ganges to cool us, family and friends at our side."

It is the "family and friends" circle that helps the businessman. He usually does not borrow from the banks or finance company. It is his friends and relatives who give him 20 to 30 thousand pounds. He then either buys a shop or starts a small manufacturing unit. When beginning his business the writer was advised by an indigenous old retired director "Trust nobody". An Asian's start, on the other hand, is always with a "Trust" in his friends and relatives.

In certain businesses, an Asian helps an Asian. We still have the elements of a tribal society. We have come from a background where men used to help with each other's harvests. Dairy businesses and innumerable pub businesses usually have Asian customers.

While Asians these days are moving into other fields, the most well-known are in manufacturing and or sale of garments and in food stores. There are as many as 700 or 800 garment manufacturers in the Midlands. There are about 250 in Birmingham alone. It is said that if you ever lose your way in Hockley or Smethwick, you will come across an Asian garment manufacturer. There are 50 or 60 in the city of Wolverhampton.

I do not claim this to be an exhaustive study of Indian businessmen in the Midlands. What I have tried to put forward are the reasons that contribute to their success in their respective limited fields.

Lastly, there is a hidden store of goodwill in this country. It is our job to find it, harness it, and use it for our own betterment. The writer received unpaid assistance from a retired Englishman who brought over 35 years' experience in Black Country metal finishing to bear on the company's techniques and gave advice on plant, machinery and materials. We will always remain indebted to the 'Saint Adviser' and his home is always a shrine for us. In a nutshell, for every door that is closed, there are a dozen open. We, the Asians, therefore are confident that within 15 to 20 years, we will reach heights that our forefathers never ever dreamed of.

Let me conclude with a bit of self-appraisal:

"Brave men are we, and be it understood,
We left our country, for our country's good
And none may doubt our immigration
Is of great value to the British nation."

Our advisor, the late Gwyn Thomas of Pelsall, West Midlands.

Poet and Politician Edmund Waller (1606-1687).
Old Age

"The seas are quiet, when the winds give o'er,
So calm are we, when passions are no more.
For then we know how vain it was to boast..."

Written in 1991

The River of London

The writer on the River Thames in 1995. Photo by Dr Gurbachan of 'FILHAAL Punjabi Quarterly', Chandigarh.

At times it looks like "Ravi" and at others "Jhana" – this river of London.

Anybody can have a ride on the river while he is alive, but only the chosen few when they are dead.

Queen Elizabeth I firmly established English supremacy after defeating the Spanish Armada. England became the pre-eminent sea power and established the British East India Company. Spenser, Marlowe and Shakespeare created literature. The period of the Queen's rule was called "The Golden Age". Hence, as a symbol of respect and honour, her dead body was afforded a funeral journey upon the Thames.

The empire was established during Queen Victoria's reign. She was hailed as the "Queen of Waves" and the "Queen of the world". Science, literature and industry set up milestones to honour Victoria on her final journey on the Thames.

The river of London does not honour only the Royals but also the warriors and the martyrs of the nation who are equally as dear to the people. Their memories are celebrated by organised fairs or, permanently, by statues. The body of Lord Nelson, the hero who

Queen Victoria (1819-1901)

fought heroically both on land and in the sea against Napolean, was displayed on the river bank for three days. Afterwards, his dead body was also made the river journey, in royal grandeur, for burial. These events were engraved on the memories of the contemporaries like a line on a brick. A monument, 156ft high was constructed in Trafalgar Square, honouring Nelson.

Winston Churchill, who dominated Parliament for 60 years and died at the age of 91 in 1965, was given a state funeral, the first for a non-royal since 1914, and part of his funeral route was via the Thames.

However, I cannot imagine anybody in the Royal Family in the 21st Century being given a funeral on the river route.

Outwardly, the Thames appears to be but one river but it is in fact a combination of 14 smaller tributaries. We find a reference to seven or eight of them in English literature almost 900 years old. Many of these rivers still flow under our feet or tyres, mostly underground through huge pipes.

Some have dried up while others are hidden and others get re-vitalised. The world famous Fleet Street, once the home of English Press, was only a river. At one time, the Fleet was a mere 13ft wide (in Hampstead) but it spanned 600ft at the time of the Roman conquest of England. It was also called "Hole-bourn" – the "river of the well" or the 'river of streams'. This was the most important among the list of lost rivers.

Two rivers no longer in existence, called Effra and Westbourne, were used to power at least two dozen flour mills.

The Wallbrook flowed up to 1598 and it had been only a huge dirty pond during Roman times. When the Romans built the Wall of London, the river ceased to flow. It went under ground near the present-day Bank

Queen Elizabeth II Bridge

of England, where it was seen re-awakened in 1732 and 1803. According to the bank employees, you can still feel its flow in the foundations of the bank.

The City of London is at the lower end of the Thames valley. There are springs around the city and especially on the north side. The water of these springs is sweet and clear The areas of Hollywell, Clerkenwell and Saint Clementswell were named after these springs. During the glory days of Oxford and Cambridge Universities, the youth and scholars alike would come out to these springs for relaxation. Instead of sipping pint after pint of beer, as they might do today, they nourished themselves on these springs.

In the north, at a height of 400ft are the hills of Hampstead and Highgate and south of the river are valleys and lofty hills. At a distance of about every three miles in this area, you will find a small river that merges into Thames. The central part of London was created as a result of the flooding of these small rivers towards the down slopes. This is a stretch of about two or three miles. After that the river again flows with vigour and speed.

You cannot see these small rivers. They have been merged with each other under ground in the middle of the city of London. Sometimes it becomes difficult to find the differences between the hidden part of the river and a small flowing river. Much concrete has been used to contain the Thames in London but it is very difficult to hide the river Wandle, which is seen to some extent near Wandsworth. The use of cement and concrete can annihilate these rivers for good.

The Thames has the same importance in the history of England as Whitehall and Westminster. This is the main artery of London's heart, the gem of the empire.

We cannot speak of London without mentioning Thames. This river existed before the birth of London. The city came into being because of this river and the Romans who chose to settle near to it. The beautiful waters reflect the change of seasons as well as the time of day – dark blue in summer, silvery in the evening. When frozen in winter, the river is like a shining, polished stone. People roast chickens on it, cycle on it and organise fairs on it.

The river is London's most civilised and beautiful route. Few experience the impatience often characteristic of road travel when journeying on the Thames. It is one of the world's friendlier rivers.. People from all walks of life of all ages and all nationalities visit it. It attracts with equal gravitational force the farmers, the workers, poets, peasants and the artists. Queen Victoria and Prince Albert, against the advice of the Royal seniors, celebrated their honeymoon on the river, such was its attraction. Many powerful aristocrats built their homes along its banks, often after demolishing village after village. One cannot know how many marriages it has witnessed. People gravitate to the banks of river in Hammersmith in the same way pigeons flock to Trafalgar Square.

Rivers have much importance in the history of mankind. The Thames is also one of the most influential. Rivers such as the Nile, the Sindh and Euphrates virtually created the ancient civilisations and, in fact most of the famous cities of the world came into being due to their rivers. Banaras, Delhi, Agra and many other big cities of India flourished because of their rivers. King Porus of Punjab challenged Alexander in between the rivers of Atak and Jehlam.

The Seine in Paris is famous for its beauty. The Danube that passes through Europe is no less attractive. Budapest in Hungary is situated on the Danube and the Cologne in Germany is on the Rhine. The Praha divides Prague into two. Young couples make love on its ancient bridge.

Rome is host to the Tiber.

The river Dijlah divides Baghdad and Basra gets divided by the Furat. Every evening, when the beautiful Queen Cleopatra would come out on to the waters of the river Nile, the people of Cairo would be transfixed when the river water was set on fire by her beauty. To this day, rich oil magnates still go out on the Nile like Cleopatra.

Canberra is the capital of Australia though the country's largest city is Sydney. Why is the city of Melbourne so beautiful? Perhaps it is because of the Yarra river!

River Vltava in Prague

The beauty of the Thames is not due to the Tower of London alone and not even to the royal palace of Hampton Court. Rather, we are more impressed with the magnificent buildings because they are on the banks of the river. The Thames is the meeting point of power, national pride, St Paul's Cathedral and places of entertainment.

From an aristocratic viewpoint, Hampton Court is the most magnificent, where no fewer than 1,000 guests can relax into the night. In its garden the laughter of the children who play hide-and-seek is worth listening to. Ham House and Orleon House are gems in architecture. There are many parks and houses on the banks of the river. In 1905, an Indian named Rattan Tata created an edifice which was the pride of this river. People still come to see a fountain which he installed at York House in Twickenham. The exiled family of the emperor of France once took refuge in one of Tata's houses.

For about 900 years, Fulham Palace was the residential home of the Bishop of London, up to 1973. This house may lack aristocratic glamour but people still visit its ancient garden. The joggers' favourite part of the Thames is St James Palace, the symbol of London. It has been on the river for centuries, as has the Buddhist shrine.

Scotland Yard, the headquarters of MI5, Parliament House and the residence of the Archbishop of Canterbury since 1190 are all close to the Thames.

HRH Princess Diana (1961-1997)

The foundation of Christianity in 635 was done on the banks of the Thames. It took 400 years to build the sanctuary abbey in Dorchester.

At Kew, which is on the banks of the Thames, there are 200-year-old gardens in 300 acres. Next to that is Chelsea Physic Garden. Plants used in medicine are grown in abundance here.

Chelsea Harbour is the newest place for young lovers

Main Hall of The Pensioners Royal Hospital, Chelsea

to walk around. There has been constructed a giant globe, where sailors can easily see the tidal pressure. An artistic shopping centre and a hotel are quite clearly visible, but the car parks, which are like cellars underneath the river waters are invisible. Princess Diana used to do her gymnastic exercises here. At Docklands, there is a 25ft high tower – the highest in England – near the sea. The Cutty Sark lost its rudder and

Chelsea Pensioners

came into port in 1872 a week behind the winner Thermopylae in one of the tea races to China. The Cutty Sark is now permanently docked at Chelsea Harbour.

Chelsea Harbour also has on display hundreds of swords, as well as medals won by their generals. The names of 250 soldiers who were killed by Sikh soldiers during the Sikh wars of Maharaja Ranjit Singh are engraved near the ex-servicemen's hospital in Chelsea. Thousands of haughty Sikhs residing in England tried to disparage them but never think of erecting such memorials in their mother country where their brothers laid down their lives defending their Punjab. It is easy to see how governments evaluate their martyrs by the way they honour their dead. Londoners always respect their veterans by bowing their heads to them. There are 20 flags displayed high on the walls in the entrance hall of the church, including those of Shivaji Marhatta. Instead of looking up to them for a long time, you start glaring at your own uprooted feet (in despair or shame).

In Westminster Abbey is the tomb of dramatist Ben Jonson, who, along with other dignitaries, preferred to be put in his grave in an upright position to save space on the island of Great Britain, which is already too small.

Almost two centuries ago, in 1832, there was a cholera epidemic in London, due to the dirt disposed of in the river, and 14,000 people died. An engineer, who was living in Cheyne Walk built a drainage system 1300 miles long, which is still the backbone of the capital. The water is filtered and fertiliser is prepared from it. Only clean water is returned to the river.

If the Himalayas are the defence of India, then the Thames is the motorway of the invaders. They always entered Britain via the river. Even now, you can always see a few helicopters patrolling the river. The Huns, the Vikings and later on, the Romans entered Britain through this route. The Romans even built the Great Wall of London and crossed the river near London Bridge with a wooden bridge. Then, after constructing a network of roads, they ruled over England for well over 300 years. The river was an artery for the strong, the invaders.

Tilbury, or London, is still perhaps the biggest port in the world. The Thames is not just window dressing or a means of entertainment only. This is a route which has been used for centuries and people have availed themselves of it. It may be a decorative waterway after Putney Bridge. If you see somebody on the bridge, it won't be like the Seine in Paris where people just cross the river to go to work.

For Londoners, the river has been a source of food for centuries. You find 114 types of fish in it, including salmon. Battersea and surrounding areas are called "the heaven of fish."

It is not only riverboats which add beauty to the river at night but also the many bridges. Tower Bridge has been well known all over the world for decades. The twinkling Albert Bridge, at twilight looks magnificent, as if the Indian ministers are decorated with garlands of varied flowers.

Some of the bridges are built with cemented pillars but others are of swinging type. Such bridges could go out of line if they get shaken. That is why heavy loads are forbidden to use them. Even the soldiers, with their heavy footsteps, are not allowed to walk on them. They have been instructed to cross it with soft steps, on their toes only, and also to stop at times. Such bridges have now been fortified thanks to modern technology.

Sometime, even the charities make full use of these bridges. Money for the Stroke Association is collected by about 500 cyclists who use a route which takes in 25 Thames bridges.

There are many fairs and events held in London and one of the best-known is the boat race between Oxford and Cambridge Universities which dates back to 1829. The distance is only 7 miles and 374 yards and has been covered in 17 minutes. People leave the comfort of their homes and their television sets and come in thousands to see the race. They sing songs and then they flock towards the race to encourage the rowers. In Victorian times, people would come to the site a week before the race. There was a fair from Chiswick Bridge up to Putney Bridge. People would come very enthusiastically to encourage the rowers. Some would take their own boats to follow the race and roar on the crews like camels on the river surface.

Longer boat races are held as well, in which the fastest finish in 24 hours while the slower participants finish in three days. A race called "a canoeist's Everest" is 125 miles long.

The British neither deny their ancestors' traditions easily nor do they take it as an insult to be disciplined. There is a tradition in London since 1422 that the mayor of the city must take an "oath of allegiance" before the king or queen. This is part of what is known as the "Lord Mayor's Show."

To say farewell to the 20th Century, such a show was planned on the Thames and took place inside the Millennium Dome. It was not a new tradition. Such shows were held on the highway of the Thames even before that. It did not obstruct traffic and people were entertained as well. Thousands of well-cared-for and well-decorated boats could be found on the river. Every company would have their own colourful uniforms. Thus boat traffic was increased and navigation became narrower and narrower. Boatmen raced their boats, resulting in fierce competition that sometimes led to fist fights. The courts flourished.

On the Thames are birds which are otherwise well-bred, tailless, heavy-footed and with longer necks. They are called "grebe" – poor – in English and are very good at diving. Sometimes they carry their young piggy-back style. The young ones move to the front and the elders to the back like cattle grazers, a type of tribesman who tends sheep by urging them forward. They move forward like soldiers – straight ahead.

There are also swans here. These birds are somebody's property and are looked after properly. They belong to either the Royal Family or are owned by two other companies. Like the boat races, these birds are displayed on the river in a fair – a sort of procession. It is called "swan–upping". This presentation is much more colourful than the boat race held at approximately the same place.

July and August is the time for listening to bird songs. It is their mating season. Sparrows are found here but the kingfisher is the Cleopatra of the river, having the most beautiful feathers of all the birds there. Pigeons may fly in the morning but seagulls go on long all-day flights. These birds are the ornaments of the Thames. There we see white seagulls, flying like a group as sparrows, as well as ducks.

The banks of the river are full of flowers and history. There is a Roman wall in Gloucestershire where T.H. (Thames Head) is written. This was only a water fountain but some people consider it the start of the river. It then becomes a lake. Here, 1800 years ago, Roman soldiers must have drunk water from the pitchers of the women taking home the spring water.

Researchers have counted more than 1100 types of flowers around the banks of the Thames which are used in medicine including the treatment of cholera. In the hotels and lounges of Londoners, these flowers do not look as magnificent as they do on the banks of the river in their natural setting. Like a crop of mustard flowers, the image of sunflowers is very pleasing. Flowers which are in the marsh are perhaps saying "Cheer up, comrades, I've survived through the winter." However, along with the various beautiful flowers, we also find a

Thames Barrier

poisonous and vicious flower called ragwort. Even cattle are fearful of it and if not controlled it spreads like wildfire.

Once, the Thames was flooded by a very mischievous and vicious high tide. Material loss was great and it took 300 lives as well. It happened in 1953 and before that, in 1928, London lost 14 people in a similar incident.

In certain unfortunate places of the world, it is still difficult to avoid flooding of small streams or rivers, but after this event London accepted the challenge and closed the river mouth forever from the sea. They built four big and six small doors at Woolwich like the doors of the fort at Fatehpur Sikri. Initially these doors were only 5ft high but afterwards the height was increased to 65ft each. They spent £500m in 1982 and people can sleep soundly now. Within half an hour of the news of a high tide, these doors shut as if London's river is accepting the challenge of the sea. It is easy to save the Thames from flooding. The wild tide of the sea is disciplined wherever it creates danger. Thus, they save their citizens from natural calamity.

A horse creates havoc if he is not well trained. However, when the horse is properly trained a man rides on it. London has trained its river in such a way that it cannot create panic among its people. It is like a snake charmer who can put a snake in a basket. The Thames Barrier of Woolwich was the answer. The river then looks like a puppet that can be controlled. The barrier is the biggest in the world and can be rented out and taken to any part of the world. Last year it was raised for the 30th time, when London received news of Hurricane Lily. Had it not been raised in time, losses costing billions would have occurred. The underground railways would have been flooded and for about half a mile from the West End all the cellars to the buildings would have been under water.

Richmond island of Vancouver and Andaman Nicobar and the Lakshdip Islands of India are subject to tidal fluctuations. Similarly, London could be under water in 100 years. There are two reasons – the level of the North Sea is rising every minute and the bedrock under London is giving way. Satellite surveillance has been set up from Richmond to Southend which will show the distance lost every year. In this way, a solid barrier to save London could be built 100 years in advance of the fall.

The great beauty of the Thames has been neglected for many years. In order to enhance the glamour, new buildings will be built, while others will have glass roofs. Art works will then be displayed. A cable car may even be installed from Covent Garden to Festival Hall.

The British are far-sighted. After discarding unworkable ideas, they follow new thinking. Backward parts such as Southwark will be connected with the affluent part by a new bridge. Even apartments could be built on the bridge, as well as a light railway.

There is a pool near Venice which is called "Lido". After spending about 15 to 20 millions, London is planning a floating lido on the river. It could be residential and people then could enjoy the river on days and nights. The capital would then be the Venice of North. Riverboat traffic could be started and the Thames enjoyed for more than just observation.

Londoners are repenting after losing their dead rivers. They still wish them to be revitalised. For example, Farringdon Road could again be converted into the River Fleet. It requires huge changes but it could then rival Canal Street in Amsterdam.

The main artery is already clean and clear. After revitalising the other rivers, more arteries will become clean as well. London will become the Land of Five Rivers just as Punjab means the land of five rivers. The Thames could then say:

"Millions of Alexanders have ridden on my breast,
Thousands of flowers have blossomed and faded on me,
Rivers always flow to the sea,
We'll carry on flowing,
We'll carry on moving."

Written in 1996

An Exchange of Letters with an MP

Mrs Jaswinder Kaur and her husband Mr Satinder Singh in Wolverhampton.

The Asian community in Britain is indebted to their beloved MPs, who off and on helped them in getting settled here.

The Right Honourable Dennis Turner, now Lord Bilston, once joined hands with two other MPs – Piara Khabra of Ealing and Ashok Kumar of Middlesbrough – to help the writer and eight of his friends from the Asian community in the Midlands.

We are equally thankful to two late Conservative MPs – first, Enoch

Powell and his successor Nick Budgen. The former, after quoting the Roman poet Virgil – "Wars, terrible wars and the Tiber foaming with much blood" – predicted race riots in 1969 and after a decade the latter accused the first generation of Asians of "selling their daughters to the highest bidders."

This writer asked Mr Powell a number of critical questions when he finished his speech in St Jude's school, Wolverhampton, and wrote an open letter to Nick Budgen which was published in *Des Pardes Weekly* in January, 1976, and later circulated to many other MPs and people in power.

The readers may excuse the writer for some of the language which he used about four decades ago but people still believe that the exchange of these two letters did create positive impressions on both sides. Mr Budgen, in his later years, helped a number of parents in getting their blocked fiancés to enter Britain, including this writer's niece and her turbanned fiancé.

Enoch Powell MP (1912-1998).   **Nicholas Budgen MP (1937-1998).**

An Open Letter to Nick Budgen, Conservative MP for WolverhamptonSouth West

Dear Mr Budgen,

You have claimed that Asian girls already in this country are being sold to the highest bidders in order that their fiancés could enter Britain.

Aren't you, Mr Budgen, misguided or mistaken in this respect? We know the man who backbites the Asian community and in that light, we advise you to remain careful of him. If your guide's name starts with the letter 'N' or 'S', then you should immediately reconsider the statements that you have made in the Press, failing which, please give us proofs of your allegations.

Your statement, Mr Budgen, reminds us of the patriarchal family of early Rome. The Roman pater familias was not merely the domestic head of the family, he was the priest, the ruler and the supreme lord of his

Lord Turner of Bilston
Vice President - J.W. Hunt Cup

Lord of Bilston Dennis Turner.

people. His power over the family was absolute. He could punish his children, disown them, sell them or dispose of them in any way, even by killing them. Haven't you, Mr Budgen, had a dream of the Roman Empire in Britain and out of that frightfulness accused the Indian father of selling his daughters to the highest bidder?

Ours is a father-right family. The father is the head and functions only as a manager and not as the Roman pater familias. He is the administrator of the family, to him all persons living under his roof such as his unmarried sons and daughters are subordinated. But in respect of arranging a marriage, he always consults his wife, his relatives and other kiths and kins. Partly through traditions and partly through his own experience, the father selects the most suitable partner for his children.

We also do not believe in 'Hollywood Marriages', Mr Budgen, which means love at first sight and divorce at the other. It is in the interest of the stability of the marriage that we prefer Indianised fiancés from India.

The basis of an Indian marriage is, perhaps, love and sacrifice. Sita, Savitri and Mandodri are the classic examples of love and sacrifice. The adjustment of the partners to one another through the tensions and crises of the family cycle is imposed by social pressure and social control which, we believe, leads to harmonious family relations.

Do we, Mr Budgen, belong to the nation of shopkeepers? Certainly not. We are the off-springs of simple-minded, unsophisticated peasants. Believe us, we rather work hard than make money by mean methods as you have pointed out.

We are not the Andaman Islanders, The Pygmies of Malay, the aborigines of South Australia, the Bushmen of Central Africa or the so-called Red Indians. We are the Indians, with a few years' civilised history at our backs.

But on this side, the picture and traditions are different. Young women must try to insinuate themselves into the good graces of young men by desperate

Dr Ashok Kumar (1956-2010), MP for Middlesbrough.

121

Piara Khabra (1921-2007), MP for Ealing, London.

means. And if they are ugly they become veritable butterflies. One is living not far from my house. The call of motherhood sounds loud and clear within them. But they cannot have these blessings until they find favour in the sight of men. Can tyranny go further, Mr Budgen? No pen can describe the anguish of these women who cannot find purchasers. They are stranded and none pities them. They become human wrecks, the refuse of the market. Can you, Mr Budgen, point out just one single Asian girl, whom we as parents have deprived of motherhood?

Your supporters, Mr Budgen, are also "unable to understand why these girls do not join their future husbands in their country of origin". If they explore a bit of history, I may say, the answer becomes quite clear.

With the war of Plassey in 1757, the British rule in India began with outright plunder. All this resulted in the famous famines of India. The working class became unemployed and died in tens of millions.

Not only that, this was followed by rigorous attempts to restrict and crush Indian manufacturers by various means and internal duties. The Indian textile industry collapsed and Lancashire, where our fiancé is to come and work, became the centre of the Indian textile industry. The raw cotton was grown in India, cloth was manufactured in England and then sold back to India. This policy continued throughout the 19th Century, breaking up other old industries – ship-building, metal working, glass, paper and many crafts. Now, you John, you Mr

Lawrence and you Mr Bull, tell me honestly what course of action will your fiancé take under such circumstances?

Compare yet another thing, you Mr Budgen and also Mr Lawrence. No American fiancé longs to come to this country as an immigrant. The independence of the States is more or less contemporaneous with the loss of freedom in our country. Surveying the past century and a half, an Indian looks somewhat longingly at the vast progress made by the USA and compares it with what has not been done in his own country. If your forefathers, Mr Budgen, had not taken this great burden in India, as well as they tell us "endeavoured for so long to teach us the difficult art of self-government" we and our fiancés would never have even spilled on this mother country of the crumbling Commonwealth.

In the light of these facts, you, therefore, need not expend all of your indignation on Indian fathers. All this cant about man's respect and love for the girls in this country is completely untrue.

In coming from India to England, a girl changes her geographical position but not her social position. At the end of the Women's Year, you have put a slap on the face of an English woman as well. It is a pity that no indigenous women's organisation as yet has raised a voice against it. We need a Florence Nightingale or a Caroline Norton to plead the case of their Asian sisters.

Now you tell me, Mr Budgen, what will your girl and your fiancé do in a land which has already been plundered by our forefathers? The very word 'loot' belongs to my language but has become a part of your language, because your forefathers looted us to their fill.

Some of your statements about 'Norton Villiers' in the Parliament were remarkable and patriotic. But it just does not behove the 'great', the 'Sahibs', the 'civilised' to throw baseless mud on the strangers. There is, we know, a hidden store of goodwill in this country and despite adverse propaganda, we are confident that we shall find both the goodwill and the will to get our fiancés here. Mr Budgen, believe us that.

Yours sincerely,

Manmohan Singh Maheru

Reply from Nick Budgen MP

5th January, 1976

Dear Mr Singh Manmohan,

   Thank you so much for your long and, if I may say so, very well argued letter. I will attempt to answer the points which you raise. I hope you will forgive me if I enclose a copy of each of the two speeches to which you refer.

   In your second paragraph you ask me for proof of my allegations. I repeat that I regard my sources of information as confidential. But I must say that I regard your letter as confirming my suspicions. You say:

1.   *That the system of arranged marriages is widely used by the Asian community resident here.*
2.   *That there are considerable financial advantages for an Asian male coming to work here.*

   It is not a very big logical step to say that some fathers will abuse this situation by taking money for arranging a marriage with their daughters and thus conferring a right of entry upon the male fiancé.

   The right of entry to male fiancés was given because in a Western love engagement, it is widely believed that the separation of persons who hope to marry causes hardship and suffering. Plainly in an

124

arranged engagement or marriage suffering is not caused if the parties cannot marry.

You argue that arranged marriages supported by the traditions and customs of the Indian community may produce more stable marriages than love marriages – that may be so. But I do not believe that an arranged engagement should provide the basis for entry into this country, which is overcrowded and has many problems in the areas into which immigrants come.

Thank you for the summary of the relations of our two countries of origin. I come from a family that has for generations worked in the Commonwealth. I accept that the British people have some obligations to the Commonwealth. But surely a British politician must be concerned first of all for the people of his own country?

I accept that in the course of the British rule of India some injustices were done by the British to the Indian people. But I find your argument that most of India's present problems were caused by the British somewhat exaggerated.

I hope that on reflection you will agree that good race relations depends upon the maintenance of a strict control of the rate of immigration into this country. Your desire to allow fiancés to continue to come, if necessary, in large numbers puts good race relations in jeopardy.

Yours sincerely,

[signature]

Nick Budgen.

A Glimpse of the Languages
of the World

Arriving at Heathrow Airport.

Britain, the mother country of the Commonwealth, is a multi-racial and multi-cultural society. After the war, but especially in the Sixties, people from different parts of the world were welcomed to England. Those who came and settled brought with them their own languages. Those such as German, Punjabi, Turkish, Gujrati, and Hindi are not the official languages and therefore have limited importance in Government circles. Nevertheless, these minority language communities such as Indians have a concern about preserving their mother tongue in Britain. It is their hope and wish that these languages be taught in British schools as part of their children's curriculum. It is, in fact, a question of language survival (or survival through language) that we want to examine here. In order to do that, we should divide our project according to different categories.

1. Many Languages in the World – a General Survey

Although there are more than two and a half thousand different languages spoken on the planet today, they are divided into 12

A scene of Sikh and Christian scholars who met in Ludhiana, Punjab to translate The New Testament in Punjabi.

127

Dr Samuel Johnson (1709-1784), the acclaimed author who edited the first English dictionary.

Bhai Kahn Singh Nabha (1861-1938), who edited the first Punjabi dictionary.

fundamental language families and 50 lesser families. English belongs to one of the 12 most important, the Indo-European family. The importance is a function of the number of speakers of that language around the world.

Indo-European is thought to have originated about twenty-five thousand years ago in central Europe. If a century can see four generations, this means that one thousand generations have occurred in an unbroken chain since the beginnings of this language group. The speakers of the original language would find it impossible to understand what the language evolved into, due to the endless migrations across the face of our planet. However, there is a common word that has been suggested as a common link between all primitive Indo-European tribes. This word is the word for ox yoke.

In addition to the over two thousand separate languages spoken today – according to the French Academy – there are many thousands of dialects. Figures range between seven thousand and eight thousand known dialects and there may be many languages in remote areas that are essentially unknown outside that area itself.

A dialect is considered a variant of a primary language that has sufficient differences in idioms, pronunciation or vocabulary to make comprehension difficult if not impossible in many instances to someone who does not speak that particular dialect. One such

Sir Richard Temple, an English scholar who helped a lot in collecting and publishing Punjabi folklores. Punjabi folk-tales reflect our wisdom.

example that comes to mind is the Spanish language as it is spoken in southern Spain versus the "Spanglish" present in the ghettos of east Los Angeles, California. Another is the English language, not just as it is spoken in America versus England but as it is spoken in Californian as opposed to Oklahoma; or in Bristol as opposed to the Geordie of Newcastle-upon-Tyne.

Over 700 languages are spoken in sub-Saharan Africa. Hundreds more exist among the indigenous tribes in the jungles of the rain forests of Brazil, in South America, some that are virtually unknown outside a 100-mile radius of the tribe. In India alone there are 18 official languages and hundreds of minor ones.

Although the entire Bible has been translated into approximately 275 languages, specific sections have been translated into close on 2,000 different languages.

When a government conducts most of its business in a particular language, that language is recognised as "official". For example, in the United States, the United Nations has six official languages – English, French, Spanish, Chinese, Russian and Arabic. Perhaps this has something to do with all of the above countries having access to nuclear weapons, perhaps not. In any event, there are more "official" languages in the geographical area formerly known as the USSR than any other place on earth. There were 15 republics each with its own language, back in the day, plus various associated republics within the larger one which in turn had their own language as well as their own alphabet. In the Caucasus Mountains, the region from which Gurdjieff hailed, there were at least 80 separate languages spoken within a relatively small area.

An Indian Rupee, with dozen or so different scripts of eighteen languages.

The Aborigines of Australia, although fewer than 60,000 in number, speak more than 200 languages. As the tribes disappear, so do the languages.

There are only 101 languages spoken by over a million people in the world today. The 14 most widely spoken languages, in order of the number of speakers, are as follows:

Chinese, English, Hindustani, Russian, Spanish, Japanese, German, Indonesian, Portuguese, French, Arabic, Bengali, Malay, and Italian.

With over a billion speakers, China ranks number one. All the others have at least 50 million speakers, with English being spoken by over 300 million people. However, English is much more widely spoken globally than Chinese (as is Hindustani). Punjabi, which is a sister language to Hindustani, is the third most widely-spoken language of Asian immigrants in Britain., Hindustani itself, as the list shows, is the third most widely-spoken language in the world.

There are certain people who can be considered language savants, in their ability to learn different languages. Cardinal Mezzofanti, chief Vatican librarian in the mid-19th Century, spoke 38 languages

The first Punjabi newspaper 'Sri Darbar Sahib' - published in 1867.

and 50 dialects fluently, including certain Native American and African languages and was proficient in many others with less fluency. Sir John Bowring could speak 100 languages and understand 100 more. Vinoba Bhabe could speak all of the Asian languages of the Indian sub continent. He developed his ability through his travels throughout India.

2.   How Languages Spread and Decline

Language spreads through a number of different paths; search for food or land, through warfare, colonisation, trade or religion or some combination of the above. The principal languages spread through colonisation during the last 600 years are English, French, Spanish, Portuguese, Dutch and Russian. A language goes into decline if its base is too close to a more dominant culture. For example, England outlawed the Gaelic language after murdering the Celtic culture in the heyday of its youth. However, often the dominant language simply replaces the second language because it is more useful to the area's population. There are several states in Africa that chose a local African language as their official one but used English or French for communication in international fields because the infrastructure was already present in the form of textbooks and technical works in these languages.

Before India's independence, Urdu and Hindi, the languages of Pakistan and India respectively, were considered so similar that they were both referred to as Hindustani. The main difference between them is that Hindi is written in Sanskrit while Urdu is written in Arabic. Urdu contains many Turkish, Arabic and Persian words dating from the 16th Century. The great Mughal emperor Akbar noticed that his armies had adopted words of different troop contingents to basic Hindustani in order to expedite communication on the battlefield and beyond. He called this language Urdu, meaning "army". The word relates to the English word "horde" and essentially means a wild group, not necessarily an army.

Latin is an example of a language spread by conquest. During the time the Roman Empire covered most of the known world, the Roman language was mixed with the Celtic language and eventually morphed into the French, Spanish, Portuguese and Italian languages. For this reason, these languages are called Romance languages, not for any connotation with romance and a 19th Century conceit but for its connection with the Roman Empire.

Greek was for a time a world language, especially during the time of Alexander the Great. However, Greece was eventually superseded by Rome – some would say conquered, though Spengler takes a quite different view of the relationship between Greece and Rome – and therefore Greek was relegated to the category of culture and refinement, as opposed to the quotidian use of day-to-day business. Caesar did not need an interpreter to speak to Cleopatra, nor did Mark Antony.

The spread of Islam is an example of how language migrates through conquest by religion. However that conquest is carried out, Arabic is the language of Qur'an and thus can hardly be separated from the religion. With the rise of so-called terrorism, Arabic is being studied more in the modern era by the West than it was a hundred years ago.

Turkish was another language that came with invasions and warfare. There is a popular saying that one could travel the Silk Road, from Istanbul to Samarkand, speaking only Turkish.

3. The Study of Language – A Brief Survey

The Vedas were the first written books of the world, composed about four or five thousand years ago. The Rig Veda was written in northern

India; the mother country for the majority of immigrants who settled in Britain. For centuries men remembered them by heart, not unlike Thomas Macaulay memorising most of Shakespeare's plays. Another book written after the Vedas was the Kural, a book of philosophical wisdom about worldly affairs. The Vedas are still considered a holy book to most Hindus, similar to the way Muslims perceive the Qur'an and Christians; view of the Bible. The Veda is proof that literature was occurring on the plains of northern India as far back as 2000BC.

There is nothing new about the study of language. Men have been interested in it for at least 4,000 years. Over the centuries, scholars and pundits of India have made careful and detailed observations and analysis of their own language. Written literature, works of the poets, is available in my own mother tongue Punjabi, which was written as long ago as the 8th Century AD.

The year 1786 is regarded by many as the birth date of linguistics. In that year Sir William Jones read a paper to the Royal Asiatic Society in Calcutta pointing out that Sanskrit had striking similarities to the language of Greek and Latin and to the Celtic and Germanic languages.

Ferdinand de Saussure, a Swiss scholar who lived in the late 19th Century, has been called the father of linguistics. He said that all language items were essentially interlinked.

Others in the 20th Century also contributed to the study of linguistics, notably Bloomfield, Noam Chomsky et al.

4. Functions of a Language

The current fashionable way of describing any use of language is to say that it is used for communication. However, communication is too broad a term to be of much use to us. Dogs communicate when they

Punjabi writers Dr Deepak Manmohan Singh, Dr Ravail Singh, S. Balwant, Surinder Seehra, Dr Gurpal Sandhu, Dr Noor of Delhi and Harjeet Atwal of London.

bark or wag their tails. As Sapir pointed out, even the clouds can be said to communicate the probability of rain. However, the "language" of all these is very restricted. The word "communication" therefore should be defined a bit more narrowly if it is to be applied to human language. It can be examined in several ways.

People's native language is that of their social milieu, the apparently meaningless small talk of ordinary life. "Hello, how are you?" "Isn't the weather terrible?" "Good morning, Mr Singh, how are things?" – this type of conversation shows (a) a desire to be friendly and (b) an optimistic view of life at that moment. This conversation is socially necessary but it is perhaps not far removed from the communication of animals expressed in sounds such as a barking or in gestures such as wagging a tail. This has been called "phatic communion" by Malinowski, which is mainly polite talk, greetings and rather meaningless exchanges of words. It serves primarily to further our social

Dr Deepak Manmohan Singh of Punjab University Chandigarh with the writer, participating in a seminar.

relationships with each other. One's mother tongue can serve a beautiful purpose in this field of language communication.

Let us examine another illustration of hearing a stranger's language. Suppose you are having a walk in the evening and someone says to you "Guten Tag". You will certainly be surprised, perhaps shocked or even insecure. "Who was that to speak to me in a language that was certainly not English?" you may ask yourself. How much more the unease if the man looked Arabic or African and the language had been obviously non-European. The use of a common language assures us at least of a certain degree of social cohesion. To speak the same language is for most people a way of having a sense of security and a sense of belonging.

Even within English, the speaking of a common form often strengthens personal and social bonds. Two businessmen, both using Yorkshire dialect, may well get on better than two others, one of whom uses Yorkshire and the other Irish dialect forms. This is particularly true given the English tendency to *place* a person, to adopt a particular attitude to him, based on the form of language he uses. It is similar with Asian languages. People who speak the same dialect of Punjabi get on much better with each other than with those who belong to a distant place.

We use a very respectable and pious language at our ceremonies, which helps to make that occasion a memorable and historic one in our lives. The fertile plain lands of Northern India, in the past, used to depend on rain in agriculture. In order to please the rain god, people used to organise special rituals to pray for rain. If you see a Sikh marriage ceremony, you  will hear four special couplets or stanzas sung rhythmically. It has an almost magical effect on the marrying couple. We still believe that marriage is a pious affair and anybody who has heard those four couplets should not betray the trust and hence should not divorce either. That would be considered a positive side of learning one's own mother tongue, religious ceremonies and cultural values.

The same is true at the time of death. Special religious hymns are sung which tends to soften the desolation of life for his friends and relatives. How then can we say that one's mother tongue has no value in his life? His birth, his marriage and his death are in fact ennobled by the purity of his native language. There are many hymns or couplets which are difficult for a common man to understand but even they have a soothing effect on the eras. This ritual and ceremonial use of the mother tongue is long established in the very texture of the Asian communities which have a sort of special meaning for them. A "court registration" marriage is totally different from one arranged by the parents of Indian couples and performed in the presence of both the community and the Holy Book.

Exactly the same could be the reason for using Latin as a Roman Catholic Church language, until relatively recent times. It promotes language rather than obstructs it. Sometimes words have the power of action themselves. For example, in a Muslim country like Pakistan, saying "I divorce you" in certain specified circumstances *makes it so*, as opposed to saying something like "I am going to divorce you" or "I'm divorcing you" from a Westerner. Events could transpire that ultimately make the Westerner's statement untrue, whereas the Muslim's statement is a *de facto* event by its mere existence. In this country, Pakistan, the words of a written will are themselves actions – "I give" and "I bequeath" and so on.

Language is also used to give orders and to control other people and things. Here you need a precise and logical use of words.

We preserve our history and traditions with the help of language. No language, no history. Ancient times saw the use of an oral tradition (since the technology of the printed word was in quite a different category from what it is today) while today print, film and taped records and more exotic forms are preserved in museums and libraries.

Language is most satisfying for self-expression as well, both literature and especially poetry. It is in fact a genuine expression of humanity.

Also, to a certain extent, we are controlled in our thoughts and actions by the language we know. No two languages are identical and it has been suggested therefore that people with different mother tongues will have different responses to things based on their different languages. That is why sometimes it is difficult to translate the exact shade of meanings from one language to another.

We can say that the more flexible and wide ranging a person's language, the more likely it is that the quality of his life will be richer. Conversely, the more restricted and limited his language, the more restricted and limited his thoughts and, indeed, his life. If this is true, then certainly there is a need for some sort of language for the citizens.

If the citizens are multi-lingual, then they should be given the opportunity to learn their mother tongue and to express themselves.

5. What is Mother Tongue?

Love of mother tongue is a matter of intense emotional satisfaction. Our mother tongue gives us pleasure like music and painting. How do children learn the mother tongue even before they reach the age of four? – by continuous association of words with things and doings. It is by the use of language as a medium that every child learns to speak the language of the family, correct tense, gender and all else. Our mother tongue can be easily learned because the home is the perfect environment for learning. A person becomes richer not only by his own mother tongue but by acquiring other languages as well.

These languages, at this moment, do not have an important role in English education or in British society. Nevertheless, these languages are spoken and used in social, cultural and religious circles of their own communities. All of these Asian languages stated above have at least one weekly newspaper and at least one daily newspaper as well. Out of these, Punjabi publishes about half a dozen weekly newspapers, such as *Des Pardes*, *Punjab Times*, *Punjabi Tribune* and *Akali Patrika*.

Baba Frid (1175AD-1265AD), a Soofi poet.

6. What is a Bi-lingual or Multi-lingual Education?

Switzerland is a typical example of a country with a bi-lingual educational system. This nation has solved the language problem by having three official languages – German, French and Italian and, as if this were not enough for a fairly small country, the majority of the population uses a dialect Swiss-German, which is considerably different from standard German. There is a fourth language as well, called Romanche. The result of all these languages is not confusion, as it is on the Indian sub-continent, but rather a linguistic preparation and national concord that have made Switzerland the banking centre of the world and a peaceful, united nation of great prosperity. The multi-lingual Swiss are famous as hotel keepers, restaurateurs and, of course, bankers. It may be interesting to know that when three German-speaking Swiss are joined in conversation by a French-speaking Swiss, they immediately switch to French out of deference to the minority – a tolerant Swiss custom. The Swiss, in fact, have a saying attributed to the Holy Roman Emperor Charles V – "I speak Spanish to God, Italian to women, French to men and German to my horse."

Let us consider another example. Belgium is a country split by language. Half of its inhabitants, the Walloons, live in the west and speak French. The other half live in the east and speak Flemish, a variation of Dutch. All state business had to be conducted in two languages and the King and government must be especially careful not to favour one language over the other. In principle, everyone is expected to be bi-lingual, although each group favours its own language and there are frequent riots and threats of secession.

In deference to some of the larger language groups, Indian rupee bills contain identification in India's principal languages, including

Hindi, English, Urdu, Bengali, Tamil, Gujrati, Marthi, Telagu, Punjabi, Rajasthani, Kanarese and Malayalam.

Taking into account the stories of the above three nations, we now wish to examine how much time and energy should be spent in organising multi-language

Sir Winston Churchill. All he had to offer was "blood, sweat, toil and tears."

classes in Britain. In no case do we want to make a mess of this nation that at one time was the best in the world. We do not want to see the disintegration of the nation; not the people involved in riots and to two nation theories. Everything and anything that is to be done should be done by taking into consideration the above motive in our minds. Britain is a permissive society. Granted, Britain is trying to give equal rights and equal justice to the ethnic minority communities but in no case should we sow the seeds of chaos for the years and decades ahead.

A country, if possible, should have one central language. That is the power of the nation. It is in one central language that the king, queen or president should pass orders to the citizens and the citizens in turn should react quickly. Let us not forget history. During World War II, Churchill's use of the English language was one of the principal morale builders which enabled the British to continue their resistance against Nazi Germany when Britain stood alone after the fall of France.

Perhaps the most striking of his phrases and one that filled his listeners with pride and defiance was that all he had to offer was "blood, sweat, toil and tears". The foreign settlers and immigrants, therefore, may or may not study their own language or dialects but they must be made proficient enough in English so that if needed they can attend the call of the nation and be counted within minutes.

Not everybody is in favour of having their mother tongue taught in the classrooms of Britain. Parents know that if their children do learn their native language, it will not be of much use in helping them make a living. There are also other factors involved. A class in a second language has the added financial burden, the psychological one of demanding that children go to school for seven days a week, the size of the classrooms would give an unfavourable student/teacher ratio, the teachers or substitute teachers may not be up to the task and, finally, having the native language taught in such a way may cause a sense of inferiority among the participants.

7. Does Mother Tongue Teaching Obstruct English Education?

Bhai Mardana, Guru Nanak Dev ji in centre and Bhai Bala ji (1469-1539).

Vygotsky (1934), a well-known Russian linguist, was in favour of providing bi-lingual education to children. He felt that education in one language helped in learning another one. He quotes Goethe, the great German writer and the greatest European linguist and literary man: "Anybody who doesn't know a foreign language doesn't know his own mother tongue quite well". The European Economic Community (EEC) Directive of 1977, that stresses the need for mother tongue teaching, is based on Vygotsky's research.

International research during the last 50 years has proved positive results for mother tongue teaching. The Charter of Human Rights declares that all the ethnic minorities have the right to preserve their own individual culture and language, while the United Nations Charter for Children's Rights speaks in favour of mother tongue teaching for the children.

When a child becomes aware that poets recited poems in his own language more than 4,000 years before, and that Panini wrote the world's first and last best grammar, he feels a sense of wonder in his own roots. He feels the connectedness that helps build his self-confidence.

Let it be said here that all of this should be done with care, more on the lines of the people of Switzerland and less on the lines of the Asians who are always fighting for the survival of their own mother tongue. In doing so, they neglect the national language of the people.

West Indian children, it would seem, are more criminally minded than the Asians. Why? One of the many reasons given is that the West Indians forgot everything. They forgot their mother tongue, their culture, their religion. They were *UPROOTED*. Their lifestyles were changed to mimic Europeans rather than their own culture. The host communities compounded this tragedy by not assimilating or even accepting them. As a result, they became reactionary and often indulged in crime. On the other hand, Asian children, so far, are preserving their heritage. The teaching of their native language does not obstruct integration; rather, it creates understanding and builds up citizenship in a multicultural society.

8.   What is the Relation between Mother Tongue and Culture?

A culture is a sort of individual truth that you learn through art, music, poetry, drama, literature, mythologies and religions. Let us illustrate it through the culture of Northern Indian Punjabis. They are the largest majority of Asians living in Britain. Most of them belong to the Sikh religion. This is a comparatively modern religion, which was born about 500 years ago. The founder, Guru Nanak, created a moral spirit among the Punjabis by which they became different from the Hindus and the Muslims. Guru Nanak challenged the atrocities of the then Mughal ruler King Baber, who was collecting taxes forcibly. Guru Nanak turned his reactions and emotions into beautiful rhythmical poetry. His poems are sung every day and ennoble the lives of Sikhs. It is ecstatic; readers become genuinely carried away with it. There is a flow of powerful emotions which he composed after having a tour of the then known world.

Guru Gobind Singh ji (1666-1708).

There was a decoit named Dulla Bhatti (a rogue) in Punjab, more or less exactly the same as Robin Hood of Nottingham. Never did he say anything to the women, the poor or the weak. He became famous for looting the big, the rich, and the cruel and unjust landlords. After looting them, he used to deliver the looted money to the poor and the needy. He has become a legendary figure in our culture with many songs and poems written about him. It has become the duty of Punjabi

Came to England via Nairobi in 1964, S. Gurbax Singh Flora, President Ramgarhia Sikh Associations of GB. Very liberal and far-sighted devotee of the Sikhs.

youth to challenge the cruel or unjust people. This part of our culture is very well portrayed in our poetry by both the ancient and modern poets.

The Punjabi culture does not have the stories of slave traders or stories of one's racial superiorities, but they do have the brave legends and stories of those who faced such men. The Saint/Warrior Guru Gobind Singh is the greatest example in this field of our culture.

Let us now take the aspect of love making. We do not make love just for the sake of sexual gratification before marriage. All the girls of a Punjabi village are your sisters and you are supposed to refrain from falling in love with anyone of them. Otherwise, if you do not abide by this custom, you will sooner or later be murdered. It is an accepted morality in our culture which is preserved even in this country. You will rarely see intra-village relationships. That is, if two Punjabis in England came from the same village in India, relationships are discouraged. The stories of "Puran Saint" have become popular folklore because he refused to be seduced by his own mother – an Oedipus complex. The result was that he had become a popular hero among the Indian and Pakistani Punjabis alike. This is one aspect of our culture which we are still trying to preserve.

Take the case of Asian women. So far, most of them are not yet westernised. They are sticking to one husband and one will rarely find an Asian wife found guilty of adultery. Guru Nanak, the founder of the Sikh religion, says: "The beautiful women that you see around, consider them as your mothers, your sisters and daughters." This was the result of a reaction against the malpractices in other places and other states. Even now, a Punjabi youth may indulge in drinks but he would seldom fancy women of easy virtue.

These are only a few examples of the many sides of our native culture. Should we forget the values of our culture? Or should we try to pass them on, if possible through our own mother tongue? Not to forget one's past, not to forget one's roots gives one much self-confidence and moral power to the children of ethnic minorities, to fight back the injustices of society. The Jews, who retained and remembered their culture and language, have proved my point throughout history.

9.   Language Survival or Survival Through Language

Throughout the world, in most countries, these two aspects of language sometimes go together. Everybody loves one's mother tongue and therefore there is always wishful thinking that it be preserved.

India is a typical example of the struggle and strife among the dozen different languages of the country. So is the case in such countries as Spain, Australia, America and Canada. The last named, one of the largest modern nations, faces a possible linguistic break-up. For generations the French-speaking population of Quebec has struggled to protect their island of French language and culture against the encircling English tide, a struggle culminating in the agitation for complete separation of Quebec from the rest of Canada. One result was that French has become the official language of that province.

It has often been said, more or less seriously, that World War I was caused by street signs. All the suppressed peoples of pre-war European Serbs, Croatians, Slovenes, Czechs, Slovaks and others had the constant reminder of their subject condition in the street signs of their own cities, written in the official language of their overlords, the Austro-Hungarian, German or Russian empires.

Let us also consider the condition of language in Russia. The USSR was composed of 15 republics. Each of them had its own language as a mark of nationality. Within these republics were a number of associated republics, also based on linguistic and national groups; within these there were smaller national or tribal languages as well. Schoolchildren of the USSR were usually educated in one or two languages before they began learning the foreign languages. However, the basic message is fairly obvious: to help one's career in the republic, one must be proficient in Russian, however much one prefers one's own language.

The above argument proves the fact that in order to have a decent career one must learn English, which is the national language of this country (Britain). English is a "bread winner" language. The study of your mother tongue, unless it is a bread winner, cannot become very popular in this country.

147

Principal Bhai Jodh Singh (1882-1981), a Sikh scholar. 'The ultimate aim of this birth is spiritual.'

A majority culture and its language can usually assimilate or overpower a minority culture and its language unless it is a dominating power. Asian mother tongues teaching may carry on for ten or 20 years but afterwards you may not find students for them.

It is also possible that the economic conditions of this country may go down and the immigrant children will then start thinking of emigrating to other countries, like Canada or the USA. Only the English language will profit in the long run. Mother tongue dreams, ultimately, may just end up as wishful thinking and not a reality.

10. Conclusion – Punjabi, a Notable BEST Language; English, the Best Functional Language

From time to time in history, it looked as if a world language would be established. The hope started with Alexander the Great but he was more interested in empire than in a world language. Latin was later established by Roman conquest but could not go much further.

With the spread of Islam, Arabic also spreads and is still the national language of over 20 nations of Africa and Asia.

The Mongol and Turkic invasions of the West almost conquered the

The holy book 'Shri Guru Granth Sahib ji' pages 1439.

known world but they permitted the native languages to carry on. In the 15th and 16th Centuries, Spanish was expected to take the lead as the world language but that was stopped by the destruction of the Spanish Armada in 1588.

Waterloo put an end to French political dominance of Europe. However, French continued to be the diplomatic language of Europe, which dominated the world throughout the 19th and 20th Centuries.

German, Russian and Chinese are major languages but English is the most widely used globally.

In the last 200 years a number of efforts have been made to "invent" a world language. The most well-known, Esperanto, was invented by a Polish linguist, Dr L L Zamenoff, in 1887 but has its drawbacks in becoming a world language.

Among all the possible candidates Standard English would seem to

The Gower Memorial to William Shakespeare in Stratford-upon-Avon.

be, under present conditions, a good choice for a common world language. English has a vocabulary more than twice the size of any other language. There are over a million words and new words are constantly being added. English in its present form is used more in print than any other language. It is used in international conferences, too.

Whether or not a common world language does develop in the future, a number of major and minor languages will undoubtedly continue to flourish, kept alive by the pull of a common memory based on tradition, history, literature, national or tribal pride and love of country. A mother tongue is the total memory of a tribe or its existence. It represents the character and individuality of the group, tribe or nation to which a person belongs. In Welsh, an ancient language struggling for existence in this country, there is a proverb about language peculiarly applicable to the persistence of mother tongue – "A nation without a language is a nation without a heart."

Punjabi language is one branch of many that evolved from the Indo-European Sanskrit group. It is imperative that we must learn this language, because it opens up new spiritual vistas, which the readers of traditional literature have never been able to enjoy.

Excellent works of literature have been produced in English as well as in other major languages of the world. However, it is the fact that it was Punjabi script and Punjabi language in which became written, expressed and crystallised the world's as yet youngest major historical faith, namely Sikhism and her scriptures encapsulated poems of beauty and mortal guidance laid to rest as a teacher of the Sikh faith in "The Holy Guru Garanth Sahib."

It is this book that in the Sikh belief can lead a lost man to become in tune with the Almighty Creator.

This point places the Punjabi language on the pedestal attainable only by a very small sub-group of languages, that embraces an entire faith and lays the language down, ad infinitum, as one that the human race can cherish and love as long as it survives.

Our mother-tongue Punjabi, therefore, is the best language in the world; English no doubt is the best functional language. Why not therefore make a start by learning just one word – "WAHEGURU, Waheguru, Waheguru."

Written in 1983

In Memory of the author's Son

**Amandip Singh Sukraat Maheru
(March 1974-May 2011)**

The writer's son, the first Asian head boy of Wolverhampton Grammar School, which in 2012, is celebrating its 500th anniversary. An academic and all-round student, he was a creative thinker who strongly believed in social justice and equality. While keenly studying Medicine at Manchester he had a vision to improve the world around him and enjoyed travelling the globe and seeing real people. This led him to speak a number of languages, including fluency in Japanese, French, German and many other languages.

He also encompassed heroic adventures, once saving the life of Tobias Finke, his German friend, by carrying him for 30 days across the Himalayas.

He never made material things or making money his target in life. People were important to him. Indeed, friendliness and including those who were excluded, was his special talent that led to his popularity.

Keeping the light of his spirit alive will be memories of his extraordinary mind, his athleticism, love of learning and immense love of humankind. He championed education as well as open-minded interest in other people of the world. He could bring people together in a rare and inspiring way, whilst keeping a sense of fun alive.